The LAITY in MINISTRY

GEORGE PECK
JOHN S. HOFFMAN
editors

Judson Press ® Valley Forge

*For all who took part in and supported
the Ministry of the Laity Project*

Andover Newton Theological School

1976-1982

THE LAITY IN MINISTRY

Copyright © 1984
Judson Press, Valley Forge, PA 19482-0851

Second Printing, 1989

Unless otherwise indicated, Bible quotations in this volume are from the Revised Standard Version of the Bible copyrighted 1946, 1952 © 1971, 1973 by the Division of Christian Education of the National Council of the Churches of Christ in the U.S.A., and used by permission.

Other quotations of the Bible are from *The New English Bible,* Copyright © The Delegates of the Oxford University Press and The Syndics of the Cambridge University Press 1961, 1970.

Library of Congress Cataloging in Publication Data
Main entry under title:

The Laity in ministry.

  Bibliography: p.
  Includes index.
  1. Lay ministry—Addresses, essays, lectures.
I. Peck, George. II. Hoffman, John S.
BV4405.L35 1984   253   84-7183
ISBN 0-8170-1041-6

Preface

Most of the material in this book was prepared in connection with the Faculty/Laity Writing Project, which was, in
turn, part of the Andover Newton Ministry of the Laity Project
that began in 1976 and concluded in 1982. The editors and
all of the authors were members of the writing project team.

In a way, all in the writing project had a hand in what was
finally produced; as the papers were prepared, they were discussed at length by the whole group and then revised on the
basis of the discussion. We, therefore, acknowledge with gratitude the contribution of the following people whose names
do not appear in the table of contents but whose mark is
nonetheless upon this volume: Charles Carlston, Frank Coffin,
Penny Frabotta, Everett Goodwin, Richard Jelinek, Jack Kallis,
Max Stackhouse, Candace Sutcliffe, and Ernest Sutcliffe.

The larger part of the editorial work was done by John
Hoffman, and the secretarial chores were shared by Helen
Thompson, Sandra Van Ness, and John Morgan of Andover
Newton. Without the long hours put in by these loyal typists,
what follows would never have seen the printing press.

Finally, a special word must be said of the gracious and
persistent leadership of Dick Broholm, the director of the laity
project. He kept us going when our spirits were inclined to
sag, and we are grateful that we are now able to offer to a
wider public some of the fruits of an enterprise that was for
Dick very much a labor of love.   G.P.
                                                                    J.H.

List of Contributors

Richard R. Broholm is Director, Center for the Ministry of the Laity, Andover Newton, and a member of First Baptist Church, Hingham, Massachusetts.

Gabriel Fackre is Abbot Professor of Christian Theology, Andover Newton, and a member of Eliot Church, Newton, Massachusetts.

M. B. Handspicker is Professor of Pastoral Theology and Evangelism, Andover Newton, and a member of Newton Highlands United Church of Christ.

Maria Harris is Howard Professor of Religious Education, Andover Newton, and a member of the Roman Catholic Church.

John Hoffman is Associate with Research Team, Center for the Ministry of the Laity, and a member of Church of the Covenant, Boston, Massachusetts.

Alan Holliday is Senior Copywriter with Arnold and Company, and a member of St. John's Episcopal Church, Hingham, Massachusetts.

Carolyn MacDougall is Manager in the Switch Services Division of New England Telephone and attends United Parish, Brookline, Massachusetts.

George Peck is President and Judson Professor of Christian Theology and International Mission, Andover Newton, and a member of First Baptist Church, Newton, Massachusetts.

Jim Stockard is a Partner in Stockard and Engler (consultants for low-cost housing development) and a member of Old Cambridge Baptist Church, Cambridge, Massachusetts.

Contents

Introduction

What lies behind this volume is an effort to draw seminary faculty members into the Andover Newton Laity Project at Andover Newton Theological School. When the notion first occurred to us, it seemed to be much simpler than it later turned out to be. The idea was to have a more or less equal number of professors and laity meet regularly to discuss papers prepared especially for the group. The assumption was that papers would be written by both faculty and laity. To these papers we would direct certain questions: Is what is being said right? Does the message survive serious scrutiny? Is it genuinely helpful to the ministry of the whole people of God? Will it make a contribution to men and women trying to fulfill their ministry, especially in the work place?

Even before the whole group began to meet, we were aware that an important aspect of the process would be setting the agenda. To put it bluntly, we feared that if we just plunged in, both the subject matter and the meeting style would be dominated by the faculty members, if for no other reason than that writing, talking, and arguing are their daily meat and drink. In order to offset this potential domination somewhat, we decided to have the laity participants meet first for some sessions on their own. Nothing we did had a more profound impact on our enterprise than these sessions.

In an effort to experience the atmosphere as well as broach the themes, we held our preliminary laity conversations "on location." That is, we met in the offices and work places of some of the group members rather than at the school. How significant this was for the final result is hard to say, but there is no doubt that the "feeling tone" was different. Each session was an open, brainstorming exercise in which the laity put out for reflection the issues that were uppermost in their minds. Several different professions were represented at this point: business, government service, city planning, law. A summary of the proceedings was prepared after each session and distributed from session to session so that a cumulative effect occurred.

It quickly became evident that the range of concerns present among the participants was very large indeed. Theological topics surfaced readily, as did ethical issues. A group of themes having to do with style and attitude and spirituality kept cropping up. We moved easily from theoretical issues to practical issues and back again. No effort was made to resolve anything. We engaged only in naming matters for our attention.

The notes of these meetings make rich reading; they are daunting, too. Even a cursory glance shows that when we finally got down to business in the writing project, we were hardly able to scratch the surface of the issues raised. But from this early foray into the territory, some important convictions emerged which affected all that we later did:

1. Among the laity committed to ministry in the work place exists a great store of knowledge and insight that is, as yet, not part of the consciousness of the church as a whole. Theology, ethics, piety, and practice are all involved. If ever these treasures are fully unpacked and exhibited, the people of God will benefit enormously.

2. The *Lebenswelt,* the "life world," of the laity differs considerably from that in which the church's professional leaders live. As long as the resources of the church are prepared almost exclusively by the professionals, then in both form and content the concerns of the laity in work-place ministry will not be adequately addressed.

3. When laity take their work-place ministry seriously, they tend to find quickly that the church offers little to help and reinforce them. This is true not only of written resources but also of such opportunities as worship, preaching, Christian education, and fellowship. One of the refrains heard over and over in our group was, "We participate in the Christian com-

munity in various ways, but rarely do we find the things that really preoccupy us being dealt with. It is as if the church's leaders move in one world while we move in another."

4. Despite the "two worlds" problem, some remarkable parallels exist between ministry carried out "on the job" and ministry carried out within the body. The analysis of a secular role in terms of ministry turned up many points similar to those of the analysis of the role of, say, a church pastor or a seminary dean. It became clear that conversation across these artificial lines could be instructive for both.

With all this in the background, the Faculty/Laity Writing Project eventually convened, and the work went on for more than two years. A group of ten to fifteen, we met more or less monthly. We were fairly evenly divided, faculty and laity.

The format was not complicated. Each session dealt with a paper, which was written and distributed in advance (papers followed a list of themes and writers that had been decided upon in early organizational sessions, but the list was modified as the process went along). The writer of the paper was given time to comment on his or her work; the group was reminded by the chair of the basic questions (those listed in the first paragraph of this Introduction); and "discussion ensued." The discussion was to assist the writer in rewriting and editing the paper to be in accordance with the purposes of the project. Usually the papers went through at least two incarnations and two times of discussion.

In the discussions, certain things came up repeatedly. We had to be alert continually for the tendency on the part of faculty to take over, and on occasion we had to insist that the first part of the meeting be open only to laity comment. There were frequent problems with language. What seemed perfectly simple and straightforward to the faculty was often less so to the laity. We were made painfully aware of how "in house" much of our professional religious material is. But the spirit was almost uniformly good, and the paper writers testified to the great benefit derived from the frank, sometimes vigorous, but always affirmative critiques. Whether what we produced achieves our goals must be judged by others, but we had a grand time producing it. When we decided we must break off and get on with publishing, it was with a sense of genuine regret. We had grown together and formed lasting friendships. We had proved we could argue without falling out.

In presenting the fruits of our labors to a wider public, we have arranged the papers in the following way:

Part I explores the concept of the ministry of the laity in a reflective, though not heavily theoretical, manner. We try to make it clear that our emphasis is upon the ministry of the laity in the work place, though other modes of ministry are not to be excluded. In order to illustrate the concept, Part II offers papers in which members of the laity describe some of their experiments and struggles. We then move to examples of some of the theological issues that had been raised, and Part III gathers together three of the faculty papers on such themes. The list of topics tackled is obviously not exhaustive, and this section is meant to be more exploratory than final. Part IV relates all of this to the task of ministry itself. What lies ahead if the church takes the laity seriously in its ministry, especially in the work place? What can we do actually to implement the vision that has been emerging? We conclude with a practical chapter in which some of the findings of our five-year laity project are sketched as a guide for those who want to make a start.

As has been implied, much has been left unsaid. Indeed, probably several more books are waiting to be written by this or a similar process. We hope to have whetted some appetites even if we have not provided the whole meal.

We are very conscious that our papers address a wide variety of audiences. We decided not to edit them so as to appeal to only one kind of person, partly because there are several different groups that need to be drawn into the discussion of the ministry of the laity. We would like our work to be read with profit by laity. That goes without saying. But we want it to find its way, too, into seminary classrooms and into pastors' and professors' studies. Perhaps some of the papers can also be made the subject of church school class discussion. Better still, we wish the whole volume could be the focal point for support groups for men and women struggling to make sense of ministry in the world, whether they are ordained or not.

If in the end the vision of the ministry of the whole people of God is caught, we shall have succeeded, no matter how incompletely we may have achieved our original aim.

I.

Establishing the Concept: Bringing the Ministry of the Laity into Focus

Reconceiving the Ministry of the Laity: A Personal Testimony

George Peck

In the last three or four years my understanding of the ministry of the laity has undergone a drastic change. I might even say that my thinking about it has passed through a revolution. The results of this transformation have been many, but in particular I believe I have come to a greatly expanded vision of the church's potential for witness, a vision that has profoundly affected my own sense of vocation. My purpose in this brief paper is to share with you the story of my pilgrimage, in the hope that you might also be moved to reflect upon yours.

Let me begin with a reference to my background. My father was a coal miner in Australia. He worked in that industry for nearly forty years. During that whole time he was also a devout Christian, and for most of that time he was a deacon in our local Baptist church. There is no doubt that he brought to bear upon his life in the mines the Christian faith that he professed. He did not hesitate to testify of Christ, and in all kinds of ways his commitment to the gospel made him an influence for good in day-by-day situations, in special circumstances (such as his role in the Mines Rescue Brigade), and in the industry itself throughout the district where we lived. But my father always had within him a secret disappointment: He wanted to be a minister. He certainly was a preacher (for at least three different denominations) and a Sunday church school teacher. He was a leader in his local congregation at several important points in time. He helped raise a Christian family (his two sons were ordained and his daughter became a missionary). But as far as he was aware, and as far as his church led him to believe, he was never able to fulfill the one desire that had often been uppermost in his mind. Lacking the education and the opportunity, he had never been able to become a minister.

Not long ago, I would not have thought that there was anything strange about my father's experience. I would have taken it for granted that he was right in his conclusion about his life. God had not called him to the ministry. I, however, had been called to the ministry. I had received the appropriate training; the church had examined and supported me; and I had been ordained. I became a minister; he did not. He found fulfillment by proxy in my vocation, but he remained a coal miner and, as such, just an "ordinary" Christian.

One of the things that my recent journey has done for me has been to make me seriously dissatisfied with this evaluation of who and what my father was. He lived as a Christian where God had placed him. He made a significant impact on his environment as a servant of Christ. On many occasions he took stands and pursued courses of action because he was convinced they were required of him as a Christian. He ministered, if anyone did, to individuals, to the structures of his society, to his community. In places to which I as an ordained person could not have gained access, he was present in Christ's name, and he bore witness. The neighborhood, the organizations, the mines of our region were better because Ted Peck lived and worked there and was not afraid to minister the gospel.

Yet neither he nor his church ever thought of him as a minister or of his service as ministry. He was not acknowledged in that way; he was not specifically trained for such a task; he was not explicitly supported in what he did; he was not commissioned; he was not held accountable. Those things all happened, by the grace of God, but neither he nor his church ever brought them to consciousness or developed the programs and structures that might have made him feel throughout his life and at its end that he had, indeed, attained the status and fulfilled the function for which he had longed. He ministered without ever being able to say with clarity, "I am a minister of Christ."

My point is this: I believe that both my father and the church as a whole have been impoverished because of this state of affairs. But I had served nearly twenty-five years as an ordained minister before I realized that this ministerial dichotomy existed. What brought me to see it was my experience in the Andover Newton Laity Project. In particular it came about because of the opportunity I had to listen for long periods of time to members of the laity talk about their attempts to carry out their ministry in the secular world.

I began, of course, with ideas about the ministry of the laity, and I was influenced by ideas that we shared in the early days of the project. I had fairly strong convictions about the need for all members of the congregation to be involved in the ministry of the local church, and I had, in a general, rather vague way, affirmed the role of the laity as witnesses in their places of employment, in their homes, and in the structures of their communities. But it was not until I spent hours in conversation with some of their representatives that I became convinced that my views were inadequate.

What I lacked, I came to perceive, was a proper understanding of the specific nature of the ministry of the laity, especially as it is defined as ministry in the situations in which Christian men and women spend the bulk of their time. In addition, my concept of the ministry of the laity was seriously deficient because I had not really begun to grasp the importance of the attitude and stance of the church toward such ministry. If the laity minister in the work place, in their families, in their communities, and in society at large—if that is truly ministry (as I have come to see that it is)—then the church cannot leave the laity's preparation, support, and accountability to chance, or else something crucial will be missed. Because we had been thinking of ministry only in relation to the ordained clergy, and only, or largely, within the household of faith, we had been neglecting to a remarkable degree the church's ministry that can only be genuinely carried out by the people who are, in fact, "out there," namely, the laity.

To make myself clear, let me summarize briefly what I found as I listened to my colleagues of the laity in our long discussions.

1. My first and most striking impression was how deeply

involved laity are in their Christian lives and in questions about the relationship of the gospel to their daily work. Their minds teemed with striking theological and spiritual insight, with a vital, thoughtful appreciation for the issues involved in what they were doing as believers, all made fresher and more forceful because they came with a perspective that was different from my own "professional" outlook. I realized very quickly that, as an ordained person, I had never really learned to *hear* the laity. I had become much too accustomed simply to *talking* to them.

2. I was quickly challenged and convicted by their obvious sense that by and large the church did not take them seriously in their quest for ministry and did not support or undergird them. Since they came from several different denominations, they were not indicting just one communion. But their message was unmistakable (and all the more impressive because it tended to pour out without being particularly prompted): much of what happened on Sunday was irrelevant to them on Monday; the church was more concerned with "in-house" affairs than with their ministry in the world; they had to look beyond the church if they were to find the stimulus and reinforcement they needed to carry out their ministry in the midst of the workaday world.

3. I found it hard to avoid the unpleasant impression that, despite our good intentions, we who are ordained are often the very ones in the church who do not take the laity seriously. Nor do we always relate significantly to their real-life circumstances or to the ministry they try to fulfill in the midst of those circumstances. The very word "lay" implies a less than positive judgment, and expressions like "he's only a layman" come too readily to our lips. Here, as in other areas of contemporary experience, we have a language problem! Frequently we are dealing with people who in their major area of activity are very competent and well trained (homemakers, farmers, miners, businesspersons, professionals of various kinds), but yet we insist on calling them, in the church, "lay people." And we tend to suggest that where the Christian faith is concerned, the really important things go on *in the church*, but *not* where they spend the majority of their lives (in homes, places of employment, communities, and so on). In other

words, we project the impression that if the laity have a ministry, it is to be carried out within the household of faith, not in the world. Ministry becomes associated with only a fragment of their time and activity, and we lose our sense of the church as a whole, the total people of God, being prepared by what happens in the fellowship for what then must be done in Christ's name day by day.

4. By the time our meetings concluded, the laity to whom I had been listening became for me a microcosm of the church at large. I began to discern a vision of the church moving into the world, a vision that went far beyond anything that had ever occurred to me. I found myself wondering what would happen if our churchly agenda were to be determined by the fact that one of our fundamental tasks is to prepare, commission, support, and hold accountable all the members in their ministry between Monday and Saturday. What if we worshiped and taught and enjoyed fellowship and prayed and managed within the life of the Christian community so that for the majority of the week the laity could perceive themselves pursuing the mission of the gospel to the people and structures of the world around them? Of course, some of this had been part of my awareness all along but, as I have said, in only a rather general, imprecise way. What if I, as an ordained minister, now saw it as an absolutely basic, specific, explicit element in *my* ministry to provide resources for their ministry? What if I listened before I spoke? What if the whole church listened before it did anything—listened so as to learn what the ministry of outreach was all about, before the clergy tried to prescribe what the laity "needed"? What if, for its own upbuilding toward its mission, the church found ways to draw upon the rich store of understanding, insight, and expertise that is already there, but underutilized, in all of its members?

I have previously suggested that from my involvement with members of the laity in our project, I have been able to identify a number of issues that, I am convinced, are deeply important for the ongoing life of the church. These are not issues that I dreamed up as a professional theologian or an ordained minister; rather, they have emerged from the thinking and struggling of profoundly Christian people who are trying to minister in the world and are eager to be trained and supported in such ministry. Let me share some of these issues now.

1. *A theology of ministry.* What is ministry? What does it mean to call a secular profession "ministry"? How does that kind of ministry relate to what we now refer to as "ordained" ministry? Can any secular work be ministry?

2. *The meaning and nature of "call."* How does the concept of God's call relate to persons in secular professions? Can the church validate such a call? If so, how? How is a secular profession connected with Christian vocation?

3. *Spiritual life and discipline.* What forms of spiritual discipline are appropriate for those who are ministering in secular structures? How can the ideals of Christian character be related to the pressures of secular environments (e.g., Christian humility in an achievement-oriented culture, Christian love in exploitative situations)?

4. *The nature of ministry in institutions and systems.* How does the incarnational principle work in "sinful" structures? How does one live faithfully as a believer in such sinful structures? What is discipleship in the midst of the compromise that seems inevitable in our kind of world? Theologically, what *are* these structures in which we live and work?

5. *Christian faith and the economic system.* How is Christian discipleship related to business values and contemporary economic structures? What can we say theologically about the Western economic system, and what is the appropriate Christian response to it—unquestioned affirmation? total rejection? something in between?

6. *Christian absolutes and the problem of compromise.* How do biblical standards relate to the "real" world? What is an appropriate Christian style in a fallen system? How can Christians handle the conflicts that seem inevitably to arise between our ideals and the pragmatic demands of business, government, and the like? Are we simply left to live in two different worlds, never getting them properly together?

7. *The kingdom of God and human society/institutions.* What are the most appropriate theological motifs for understanding our situation in the world and for positioning ourselves with respect to it? How can we relate the New Testament vision of the kingdom to our ministry in the world? Is there

a doctrine of providence that is appropriate? Does God act in business? in government? Are there grounds for hope in the society in which we live?

8. *The church as the body of Christ.* What does this great New Testament image mean in the kind of society we face today? How does this "body" relate on the one hand to Christ himself (how is it *his* body in the world?) and on the other hand to the world? Is it "in the world, but not of it"? What does that mean? What is the "bodiliness" of the church in our world?

Obviously these issues are projected by people, like myself, who live and work in the Western world. Other issues are likely to arise for people in different circumstances, and the issues I have mentioned would, in many instances, have to be modified. They are, therefore, meant only to be illustrations. But please note again that they are illustrations of what is on the minds of one group of very committed laity who are trying to be ministers. I wonder what would happen if the *laos* of God, all the people around the world, could speak with their varied voices and set forth their concerns. What, then, would be on the mind and in the programs of the church? What if the whole body, including the laity within the body and the ordained, were to take with complete seriousness the ministry of the laity in the midst of the world? The challenge of that thought is the central point of the pilgrimage I have tried to sketch here.

How Can You Believe You're a Minister When the Church Keeps Telling You You're Not?

Richard R. Broholm

During the last fifteen years, I have watched Christians become excited about the possibility that they really are called to minister in their work places. I have watched them become enthusiastic as their efforts to make their institutions more just and humane succeeded. They were able to change personnel policies, to open up new options to blacks and women. They transformed hospital practices, making patient care a higher priority than schedules and routines. They enabled a spirit of collaboration to emerge between administrators and workers where before there had been only mistrust and hostility.

However, these successes were often followed by reversals. Creative suggestions were squashed. The willingness to be open and vulnerable was read as weakness. Risk taking led to dismissal. In the aftermath of these setbacks, feelings of despair and fatalism arose. The possibility of change was called into question, along with the feasibility of ministries within secular institutions. For many there seemed to be this gnawing question: How can I maintain this level of energy and sustain the personal risks when I seem to be having so little impact and when no one in the church really seems to care about what I'm trying to do?

The reason for this questioning is not as obvious as it may seem. It is more than a failure of nerve, though that may be involved. It is more than naiveté about the difficulties and complexities of institutional change, though that too is often present. More and more I am convinced that a fundamental reason why so many Christians find it hard to initiate and sustain a ministry in their work places is that they really do not believe that they are, in fact, called to ministry. In spite of sermons on the "priesthood of all believers" and admonitions to "live your faith in your daily work," the organizational and liturgical practices of the church continue to reinforce the assumption that there is no valid ministry outside the organizational church.

The thesis of this paper is that for Christian laity to act on their sense of calling and to sustain a ministry within the secular structures of society, there need to be (1) a more decisive way for the church to *confirm* that calling as a valid ministry and (2) a more meaningful way for laity to experience being *conformed* to God's will in the exercise of that ministry.

Confirmation

"To confirm is to establish as true that which was doubtful or uncertain" (*Webster's New World Dictionary*).

Our experience in the Andover Newton Laity Project underscores the fact that it is a rare Christian who is able to claim a ministry in the work place. Those few who can claim ministry often feel that their church is oblivious to that ministry, and consequently they begin to doubt its validity themselves. Their feelings are accurately reflected in this excerpt from the letter of a lay person to her bishop.

> There are two basic questions bothering me. Namely, what is the ministry of the church, anyway, and then what is the relationship between ordained and lay ministries? There seems to be a lot of confusion about both questions. . . . I haven't even stumbled on a satisfactory answer to the relatively simple question of what a priest is. I know how a lot of laymen and priests see the issue, but it does leave the nonparochial priest (or in this case, his wife) with a few questions.
>
> I guess my basic frustration is that I can't see anywhere in the Church a recognition of or much support for the only kind of ministry that I and *most* Christians can have—the daily plodding along wherever you are sort of thing, trying to offer up whatever you do to God, rarely seeing how it could make much difference. I've come to think of it as an invisible ministry because it's invisible not only to the world, but even to yourself most of the time. It's a difficult kind of ministry at best, but more so because generally it isn't even seen as a valid ministry at all, or at least that's my impression.

I am convinced that Holy Trinity's [her local church] biggest impact in this community is through the cumulative effect of individual people for whom Christianity makes a crucial difference. It's easier to see institutional programs on paper, and they may be a very good thing and are a public witness and all that, but not everyone can be involved in such programs, or can or should be a priest, or even a lay reader. So most of us struggle along feeling guilty that we are not a part of the Church's ministry, and resenting the lack of support for and utter loneliness of our own meager ministry. Surely this must be part of the alienation that exists between laity and clergy.

What is it that blocks laity from feeling confirmed and validated in their ministry?

Part of the problem results from the demands and pressures of maintaining the church as an institution. Busy pastors and active laity are so preoccupied with the program and maintenance needs of the church that it is difficult to find the energy and the time to listen to the struggle of those who are trying to relate their faith to their involvement within secular organizations. In addition, the specialized language that often accompanies each sector of institutional life persuades us to believe that helpful and meaningful dialogue is really an impossibility or would take much more time than we could possibly afford.

But neither the problems of institutional preoccupation on the part of the church nor the difficulty of communication would prove insurmountable if we could convince ourselves that this ministry to secular institutions is really a valid one that demands top priority and our best resources. So, we come full circle again. I suspect that the root of the problem lies in our unstated and usually unconscious assumption that the involvements of laity outside the institutional church are not ministry after all. For, if the ministry of laity is really important to Christ and his church, why then do we confirm through the elaborate ordination process only the ministry and call of clergy?

A friend of mine, Bill Diehl, who is an executive with a major steel company and an active churchperson passionately committed to the ministry of the laity, often will have someone tell him (usually after he has spoken eloquently about lay ministry), "You should be a minister." When he replies, "I am," the person will often counter, "No, I mean a *real* minister, an ordained one."

Everyone expects persons preparing for the professional ministry to talk about "a *call.*" We expect them to prepare carefully for this calling by studying in a seminary. Then, upon graduation, we proceed to test that call and the adequacy of their preparation. And finally, when we are satisfied on both counts, we go through a liturgy that confirms their call and gives theological validation to their intentions. If called to a local congregation, the ordained person is again confirmed in a special service that testifies to the whole community that this, indeed, is a valid ministry.

Clearly we have no similar expectations or liturgies of confirmation for laity who also believe they have a call to ministry. In fact, we accept as a matter of course the notion that laity's choice of "vocation" (laity choose, clergy are called) is based on personal factors such as skills and interests and is strongly influenced by salary and opportunities for advancement.

The impact of our current assumptions and practices is far-reaching. It is little wonder that most laity find it hard to believe that Christ has any particular interest in what they do within their secular institutions. Far from reigning as Lord over their organizations, Jesus Christ is seen as a distant and disinterested judge. He is concerned that people's behavior be moral and upright, but he is primarily focused on what is happening in his church.

Dietrich Bonhoeffer, who was hanged by order of Hitler, stands over against these prevailing notions and practices. In his *Ethics*, Bonhoeffer declares that "Vocation is responsibility and responsibility is a total response of the whole person to the whole of reality. . . ."[1] And again, "The calling is the call of Jesus Christ to belong wholly to Him; it is the laying claim to me by Christ at the place at which this call has found me; it embraces work with things and relations with persons. . . ."[2]

For Bonhoeffer, the ministry of Christian laity is clearly rooted in Christ's call, personally addressed to us at the very center of our lives. The call addresses the whole of our lives, our institutional involvements as well as our family relationships. It is in no sense a limited or partial call.

Gabriel Fackre, in a recent lecture at Andover Newton, also

challenged our status quo. He reflected on Paul's concept of the church as the body of Christ in which there are many different parts, each essential to the proper functioning of the whole body, but each clearly operating with a different set of resources (gifts) and a different role or function (vocation). The theological affirmation that in baptism we all receive our gifts and our ordination is not, he suggested, adequate to meet the crisis of nonlegitimation felt by many laity. The fact that we proceed to ordain clergy to their special calling is, in fact, a recognition of the need to confirm ministry in very concrete and specific terms.

Unless we are prepared to suggest that the calling of the religious professional is a higher calling than that of laity and is worthy of special recognition and confirmation, we must either be prepared to do away with the ordination of clergy or move to provide for the ordination of all Christians to their ministries of service in the world. It seems to me that the time has come, if we are serious about the validity of the ministry of laity, to recognize the special gifts and callings of laity and to affirm and establish their ministry in the world with the same sense of care and significance that we attach to the callings of other members of the body. Otherwise we continue to reinforce the assumption that the ministry of the laity is neither legitimate, valid, nor essential to the mission of Christ in the world. How the church can proceed will entail much careful reflection, but it is of paramount importance that whatever means of confirmation is developed be concrete, specific, and focused. Members of the laity need to be examined as to the legitimacy of their call and their clarity about gifts with the same kind of intentionality that today we focus on candidates for clerical ordination. Mass services of confirmation would, in my judgment, be worse than nothing at all.

One local congregation that has experimented with the confirmation of the ministry of laity is the Old Cambridge Baptist Church in Cambridge, Massachusetts. In the Lay Associates program, established in 1964 under the pastoral leadership of Ernst Klein, that congregation sought to ordain members who believed they were called to ministry in the world. In a statement, entitled "A Christian Style of Life in the Modern

World," the theological roots of this confirmation of lay ministry were spelled out:

> Underlying the concept of Lay Associate is a belief in the priesthood of all believers and a conviction that the worship on Sunday morning should be extended into the daily lives of the church members. Here is a small, closely-knit group of persons with an understanding of the church as mission which is having a significant impact upon the secular world and the institutional church . . . The primary function of Christian laity is perceived not in terms of volunteer labor to keep the ecclesiastical machinery turning smoothly or to maintain the physical plant. Rather, their primary work is in the world, where they are called to function in a Christian manner, making the world a more human place, a place of justice and peace. . . . If young Christians wait until they achieve a position of preeminence in their field before attempting to implement Christian ideas in the world, they will be subject to the damning judgment of the disinherited of the earth: "justice postponed is justice denied." A commitment to Christian action now may involve considerable personal risk. Without an enabling group to help make decisions, to affirm positive actions, and to give mutual support, many Christian lay persons will not take the risk.
>
> The traditional roles of clergy and laity must be reversed: the laity become the troops in the front line and the clergy, with the gathered church, help to support *them*. Until this revolution occurs, the Protestant concept of priesthood of all believers remains vague and unrealized. [3]

The church needs to provide a theologically sound way of testing and confirming the ministry of the laity that would enhance our understanding of what it means to serve Christ in the daily round and would deepen our apprehension of the gospel, saving it from a narrowly religious interpretation that stifles its power to redeem and make whole.

However, the process of confirmation, the support and validation of the ministry of the laity, by itself will not be sufficient to enable Christians to sustain ministry within and to secular institutions. Something else is necessary. Here Bonhoeffer's insight into "conformation" may provide important illumination.

Conformation

"To conform is to bring into harmony or agreement, to have the same form" *(Webster's New World Dictionary)*.

In *Ethics* and later in *Letters from Prison,* Bonhoeffer writes about the life of the Christian in a "religionless" world. While his reflections about Christian faithfulness are fragmentary and sometimes obscure, the underlying motif is that the life of faith is discovered and nurtured as people take God's world with radical seriousness and enter fully into its successes and failures. By plunging into the life of the world, the Christian learns what it means to be formed by Jesus Christ. The Christian discovers the sustaining empowerment of the Holy Spirit. Christian ministry in the secular work place is not a matter of applying Jesus' teaching and principles but, rather, is a matter of being rooted in a form of Christian piety that acknowledges and submits to Christ's intention to shape and form us in his likeness.

The word 'formation' arouses our suspicion. We are sick and tired of Christian programmes and of the thoughtless and superficial slogan of what is called 'practical' Christianity as distinct from 'dogmatic' Christianity. We have seen that the formative forces in the world do not arise from Christianity at all and that the so-called practical Christianity is at least as unavailing in the world as is the dogmatic kind. The word 'formation', therefore, must be taken in quite a different sense from that to which we are accustomed. And in fact the Holy Scriptures speak of formation in a sense which is at first entirely unfamiliar to us. Their primary concern is not with the forming of a world by means of plans and programmes. Whenever they speak of forming they are concerned only with the one form which has overcome the world, the form of Jesus Christ. Formation can come only from this form. But here again it is not a question of applying directly to the world the teaching of Christ or what are referred to as Christian principles, so that the world might be formed in accordance with these. On the contrary, formation comes only by being drawn in into the form of Jesus Christ. It comes only as formation in His likeness, as *conformation* with the unique form of Him who was made man, was crucified, and rose again. This is not achieved by dint of efforts 'to become like Jesus', which is the only way in which we usually interpret it. It is achieved only when the form of Jesus Christ itself works upon us in such a manner that it moulds our form in its own likeness (Gal. 4:19). Christ remains the only giver of forms. It is not Christian men . . . who shape the world with their ideas, but it is Christ who shapes men in conformity with Himself. [4]

Though the models for a disciplined life of prayer have been drawn largely from the contemplative world of the monastery, the reality of Christian ministry in secular life is finally dependent upon our discovering and developing a style or practice of spirituality that is profoundly "this worldly" in character, enabling us to identify with and be responsible to the world. As Bonhoeffer makes clear, true identification and responsibility is discerned by opening ourselves to the tension between being fully involved in the world and deriving our form—our ways of thinking, judging, feeling—from another kingdom that claims our ultimate allegiance.

Only relatively late in my life have I come to understand the importance, for my ministry in the work place, of a time set aside each morning for reflection on Scripture, meditation, and prayer. I began the discipline of daily meditation and prayer, not during my many years in the professional ministries of the institutional church, but at age forty-six when I began my lay ministry as a management consultant with an international consulting firm (Hay Associates). Up to that moment I had taken my prayer life for granted. I knew I should pray—I assumed most pastors *did* pray daily—but I found my activities continually getting in the way of establishing a regular pattern of prayer. (I have since come to learn that I am far from being alone among clergy and laity in giving low priority to prayer.) Though I occasionally felt guilty about the sparseness of my prayer life—especially when I was asked to speak about prayer and the spiritual life—I consoled myself with the conviction that the Lord would honor my good intentions because I was busily engaged in Christ's ministry. I now realize that my assumptions were mistaken. God does not excuse us from the call to pray, and much of my activity in church work was unconnected to God's call to ministry.

It was at the moment in my life when the church did not validate or recognize my work as a management consultant as a ministry that I was compelled to take seriously my own formation in ministry. Because I did feel called to a ministry in Hay Associates and because there was too little obvious affirmation and support for this ministry by the institutional church, I was compelled to learn with radical seriousness what it means to "wait daily on the Lord," to use the daily reflection on the Scriptures and a time of quiet listening as a means to hear what the Lord was calling me *to be* and *to do*. Surrounded by a world that carried none of the comfortable signs of the religious life, I slowly began to discover that Christ stands at the center of our life in the world where we expend most of our time and expertise. I found that he is, indeed, Lord of the world, albeit a suffering-servant Lord who redeems and reconciles the world through his apparent powerlessness on the cross.

I discovered further that the life of prayer is not so much my talking with God as it is my listening in silence. I was really not prepared for this because my models for prayer were primarily persons addressing God in some public place or liturgy. My first serious encounter with a different perspective came when I decided to spend a weekend at the Church of the Saviour in Washington, D.C. I wanted to go to the church's orientation session to learn more about how it has carried out the task of empowering its membership for ministry and mission in the world. I thought I could learn a great deal by listening to the members tell their story and share their strategies.

When I received the confirmation of my reservation in the mail along with the schedule for the three days, I discovered that the first twenty-four hours were to be spent in silence. I was irritated. I said to myself, "I can spend twenty-four hours in silence anytime. I'm spending good money and time to go down there to learn how they empower their membership, not to spend a day in silence by myself!" However, no sooner were the words out of my mouth than I suddenly was faced with the truth: Not once in my life had I ever spent twenty-four hours in silence. I simply didn't have the time for that. (Loosely translated that meant: "I'm so busy being engaged in the Lord's ministry that I can't take time to listen to the Lord.") Sobered by this realization, I journeyed reluctantly and somewhat fearfully to Washington.

In the course of those three days I discovered that the discipline of a time set apart each day for prayer, meditation, and reflection on the Scriptures is one of the keys to how the members of that small community of Christians are able to share significantly in the reshaping of their city's life and the restructuring of its institutions. Their worldly ministry is inextricably bound up with their commitment to a spiritual discipline.

Gradually I discovered that it is not so much that we meet God in this time apart, but that being intentional about the discipline of meditation and prayer is a deliberate way of tuning into God, discovering and seeing in all the events of our daily lives how God meets us again and again in ways to which we usually are not alert. An analogy may help here. I have a stereo with a station tuner that continually drifts away from my favorite classical music station. I will tune into the station and then go do some work in my study. Before long I discover that the music is not quite as clear; the sound just a little fuzzy. If I do not decide to retune the stereo, it isn't long before the music is quite distorted, and listening is no longer a pleasure.

I think the same is true for being formed by Christ. The intentional act of prayer is not necessarily the time and place when God chooses to address me. That happens in a myriad of ways and places over which I have no control. God speaks through persons and events in my life in the most unexpected ways. But if I do not seek to tune my life to God, I find that, increasingly, I am drifting and unable to hear God's voice. The act of prayer is, therefore, for me a recognition that my life is God's, that I live and move and have my being by God's grace. By my being intentional about setting aside a specific time to seek the Lord consciously, I am better able to hear when God calls. The discipline of daily meditation, reflection on Scripture, and prayer is like the act of retuning the stereo. It is an act that makes me more sensitive to God's desire to retune my life and mold me according to the mind of Christ.

Ultimately, the ability to sustain faithful ministry in difficult and lonely places is strongly aided by the church's support and confirmation. But it must also be rooted in our conviction that Christ calls us to be there, is continually present to us there, and chooses that place and space in which to form us as integral parts of his new creation. For while the process of *confirmation* is the body's way of testing, supporting, and validating our specific call, the process of *conformation* is the way by which our incarnation of that call is shaped and formed to reflect the mind of Christ.

Notes

[1] Dietrich Bonhoeffer, *Ethics*, ed. Eberhard Bethge (London: SCM Press Ltd., 1955. New York: Macmillan, Inc., 1955), p. 258.

[2] *Ibid.*, p. 257.

[3] Ernst Klein, "A Christian Style of Life in the Modern World," an unpublished pamphlet.

[4] Bonhoeffer, *Ethics*, p. 80.

Questioning Lay Ministry

Maria Harris

As a woman working in both Catholic and Protestant churches, I am often asked the question "Do you want to be ordained?" My involvement in diocesan pastoral ministry, in seminary education, and in local parishes across the country makes the question a natural one; most men in such situations are ordained. In recent years, as the churches have addressed the ecclesial status of women more and more directly, I have been forced to articulate a response to this ordination question. In doing so, I have reached the conclusion that, for me, "Do you want to be ordained?" is not really the question.

Do not understand me too quickly. Clearly, history, theology, and the practice of centuries have precluded the ordination of those of us who are women. That is a fact. Clearly, such exclusion has been discriminatory, sexist, and unfair. But just as clearly, that same history, that same theology, and that same practice are ineluctably changing. Few theologians today argue for the exclusion of women from ordination (nor should they), and in the course of time it appears likely that women of all churches will join the ranks of the ordained as they have begun to do so in main-line Protestantism. Those churches asserting an ethic of full humanity for all can allow no less.

That same ethic, however, permits a deeper issue to surface: what *form, structure,* and *shape* is the church to take even if highly selective ordination practices are eliminated? In my judgment, it is this question of church form that is the central

---

one since it points to a division in the church deeper than the one between women and men while at the same time it mirrors that division. I refer to the division within the churches of placing some into a clergy group and some into a lay group. For me, the clergy-lay division, not ordination, is the heart of the matter. In this essay, I will address that division with insights drawn from a feminist perspective.

I

Clergy-lay as an issue becomes clearer if we examine the changing shape of ministry. "Church ministry is taking an entirely new shape before our eyes, one that configures much more accurately the symbol of the eschatological people, called in the Spirit, proclaimed in the New Testament. . . ."[1] Today's ecclesiology has changed radically to focus on the entire church as a people baptized into mission. The claim to ministry as the work of all Christians is asserted around the globe. Individual churches and individual Christians are realizing that the fundamental successor to the apostolic tradition, and thus to the ministry of Jesus, is the church itself; and they are also realizing that, in contrast to an earlier understanding of apostolic succession as reserved to papacy or episcopacy, each individual Christian and each individual church must keep faith with the apostles.[2] No longer does "the church" automatically mean the ordained, the clergy; no longer is ministry seen as the exclusive work of one group.

Such understandings have led to blurred concepts regarding church office but have not always issued in the realization that crises of office are often crises of ecclesial structures.[3] My conviction is that we face the changing shape of ministry and the crises of office most adequately by addressing the organizational and social relationships in the ecclesial community,[4] especially our organization into clergy and lay. To put it more directly: if all in the church are to claim the work of the ministry, the form and shape of the church must be examined, restructured, and recreated, and the clergy-lay form may have to go.

Form is not an arbitrary organizational element. Every artist knows that form is not only the *intention* of content; it is also the actual embodiment of content. Form is based on a theme;

it is a marshaling of materials in relationship to one another; it is a setting of boundaries and limits; it is a discipline, an ordering, and a shaping according to need. [5]

Today the form of the churches in terms of their members has, in my judgment, become elitist: some of us are clergy and some of us are "lay." Perhaps a time in the past existed when this distinction was a positive one and a connotation of "higher" and "lower" did not exist; even if this connotation were once true, I do not think we can make such a claim today. Further, although we have argued for a developed theology of the laity for many decades, [6] the clergy-lay duality itself has remained basically unchallenged. (In one place, for example, Hans-Ruedi Weber muses, "I wish we knew more clearly why progress [in lay ministry] since 1945 has been so slow,"[7] without asking whether the very formulation of the issue is getting in the way of accomplishing a new vision of ministry in the church.)

A feminist perspective might shed light here. As Rosemary Ruether and others have argued, dualistic thinking—spirit or freedom versus nature, reason versus emotion, soul versus body—has oppressed women. [8]

> A revaluing of the so-called negative sides of the classic dualisms and a transformation of the hierarchical mentality is implicit in women's quest. To put it another way, women's quest is for a wholeness in which the oppositions between body and soul, nature and spirit or freedom, rationality and emotion are overcome. [9]

In this essay, my suggestion is that clergy-lay borders on being such a dualism—with "lay" reflecting the negative side, especially linguistically—a thesis to which I shall return in a moment. Here let me simply note that the division is present in our images (one is "elevated" or "admitted" to the clerical state and "reduced" or "demitted" to the lay), pervades our theology (Aquinas in *Summa Theologiae* notes that ordination conveys an active character, baptism a passive character), and limits our vision (problems of and with the clergy quickly become problems of "the church" without consideration of the small number of church members about whom one is actually speaking).

In addition to a critique of dualisms, feminism presents a

critique of language. "A language is not merely a means of communication; it is also an expression of shared assumptions. Language transmits implicit values and behavioral models to all those people who use it."[10] Feminists, women and men, have learned they can raise questions about assumptions simply by changing language and in so doing are (in Nelle Morton's phrase) "hearing one another into speech." Questioning assumptions leads in turn to questioning political structures, including the political structures of churches, and the disturbing awareness that not only are we using language but language is using us also.

> We might hypothetically possess ourselves of every recognized technological resource on the North American continent, but as long as our language is inadequate, our vision remains *formless*, our thinking and feeling are still running in the old cycles, our process is . . . not transformative[11] (author's emphasis).

II

I now wish to look at the clergy-lay division and clergy-lay language as concerns for the churches.

Let us begin with the following principle:

> If you have a group half of whose members are A's and half of whose members are B's and if you call the group C, the A's and B's may be equal members of Group C. But if you call the group A, there is no way that B's can be equal to A's within it. The A's will always be the rule and the B's will always be the exception—the subgroup, the subspecies, the outsiders. [12]

Feminists, women and men, have recognized how this principle applies to women and have caused a significant change in language (at least in the United States) by refusing to accept the argument that the generic "man," for example, applies equally to both sexes. But this example is not the only one. People from the United States who spend any time in Central or South America or Canada often begin to recognize the principle in operation when they realize that only one country in the western hemisphere (their own) uses the term "American" of itself with no qualifier; other people are Latin American, South American, Spanish American, Japanese American. Such recognition at least raises the issue of power and the question of whether a relationship exists between such usage and the fact of being a subgroup, subspecies or outsider. We have, in addition, doctors and "lady doctors," professions and "helping professions," theology and "liberation theology," education (which everyone knows is for children) and "adult education." The list is long and, in most cases, illustrates an imbalance of power, suggesting that whoever owns a word owns a great deal more. Finally, fast becoming powerful and prevalent in the churches is the distinction between ministers and "lay ministers." It is this last distinction I wish to examine at some length.

Here is the equation:

Clergy = minister

Lay, *laos*, laity (nonclergy) = lay minister

The words "clergy" and "minister" are, in practice, synonyms; if one wishes to designate as minister a person who is not ordained, one generally uses the qualifier "lay." The central question this presents is whether one can take the word "minister" and preface it with the term "lay" without at the same time placing the lay minister in a subordinate position. (Recall the principle: if you have a group, half of whom are A's and half of whom are B's and if you call the group A, there is no way that B's can be equal to A's within it.) Compounding the issue in this case, however, are the meanings given to the crucial words "lay" and "minister" in ordinary speech in the United States. The *American Heritage Dictionary* of the English language gives at least three definitions of the *noun* "minister":

1. a person serving as an agent for another by carrying out specified orders or functions (e.g., a governmental Prime Minister); 2. a person authorized to perform religious functions in a church, *clergyman, pastor*; 3. a high officer of state appointed to head an executive or administrative department of government.

The *Oxford American Dictionary* offers a similar definition: "minister" is equal to "clergyman." The same is true in *Webster's Third New International Dictionary*.

In contrast, the *verb* "minister" is not exclusively assigned to any one group: to minister is to attend to the wants and needs of others, to furnish or provide, to give aid, to serve;

to do things needful or helpful. "Ministry," the third term in the set, is somewhere in the middle; on one hand, it refers to "the act of serving; ministration" or "the profession, duties and services of a minister of religion;" on the other it is equivalent to "ministers of religion as a group; *the clergy*."

Examining the word "lay" furnishes more data. The word "layman" (laywoman is rarely noted) is unambiguous: it refers to "a member of a congregation as distinguished from the clergy"; or "one who does not have special or advanced training or skill." Even "laity," the noun, carries these meanings: "derived from lay (nonclergy)"; it means "laymen collectively, as distinguished from the clergy" (women are not noted) and "all those persons outside a given profession, art, or other specialization; nonprofessionals." But it is the adjective "lay" which is the most telling. It means "pertaining to, coming from, or serving the laity; secular; practicing (psychoanalysis) but not having a (medical) degree" and is from the Middle English *laie*, from the Old French *lai*, from the Late Latin *laicus*, from the Greek *laikos*, from *laos*, "the people" (*American Heritage*). Both the *Oxford Dictionary of English Etymology* and *Webster's Third International Dictionary* begin defining "lay" by asserting what it is not rather than what it is: lay means "not in clerical orders" (*ODEE*); "not in holy orders; not of the clergy; not clerical; not ecclesiastical" (*Webster*) and continues "also of or relating to members of a religious house that are occupied chiefly with domestic or manual work" (Funk and Wagnalls call this "menial service"), "not of or from a particular profession," "not having special training or knowledge," "unprofessional," "common," "ordinary." Funk and Wagnalls, besides agreeing with these, adds "inexperienced, ignorant and uncultivated" and concludes with the information that in cards, a "lay" hand is one with few or no trumps.

It may be objected here that such usage is mainly for purposes of distinguishing. Possibly. It may be further suggested that no onus ought to be attached to manual or menial service. Certainly. It may even be objected here that such usage, although linguistically accurate, is "only semantic" and not of major concern for the church. My first response is that semantics is never "only." On the contrary, semantics is the science that deals with meaning, and by definition, the meaning assigned to the name of any group is neither irrelevant or insignificant. My second response is a point made in another context by Paulo Freire: A person who offers such a challenge ignores what can be called the operating force of the concepts and insists on ignoring the real connotation. [13]

However, if one does want to focus on church usage and church practice, many observations are pertinent. To begin with, the ambivalence and subordination built into the term "lay" is beginning to be addressed. As early as 1964, *Encounter* published the following:

> Every specially ordained minister of the church is and remains first of all a baptized member of the church. He or she continues to belong to the laity, if this term is derived from the biblical use of the word "*laikos*," to belong to God's "laos," to God's people. [14]

But then the *Encounter* authors make the following notation.

> This theologically significant and generally accepted derivation is *etymologically probably wrong*. In the ancient church the term "laity" was most probably derived from the general use of the word "*laikos*" or belonging to the "plebs," the common, non-consecrated profane people" [15] (author's emphasis).

I am doubtful in this instance that laity was ever actually used for the entire people; although the distinction between clergy and lay may at one time have had great value, I am unaware from historical study that we have ever used the phrase "ordained laity."

Closer to our own day, the order of Franciscans known as Capuchins in Roman Catholicism have changed the name of their "lay" order from the "Third Order of St. Francis" to the "Secular Order," wishing to do away with not only the implication that the monastic model they live is the sole model of ministry but also the centuries old suggestion that being "lay" is being not in first, nor even second, but in third place. [16] However, the fact that "lay" is the correlative of "clergy" and thus partner in a divisive pair remains unexamined.

As junior partner in the clergy-lay pair and as the word that must be added to minister or ministry (as in "lay" ministry— and in "lay" school of theology for that matter), in order to distinguish it from the *real* minister, the *real* ministry, and the *real* school of theology, the word "lay" and the persons so designated are at a disadvantage, rather obviously it seems to me. "Lay" people are the subgroup, the subspecies, the outsiders of Alma Graham's principle. If "minister" without the qualifier pertains to the clergy, to the ordained, then the consequence in the church becomes clerical ownership of a sacred realm, the splitting of the world into profane and secular arenas (another distinction that might be questioned) and second-class status for 98 percent of church people.

In actual practice, of course, the correlation of lay and clergy is becoming confused because many people today exercise the roles of leadership in community and liturgy without ordination. We can go ahead for a long time with the status quo, here, but the situation may be telling us something about the way our speaking and the way our formulation of issues gets in the way of, and undercuts, a serious positive move that most church people are attempting to support—the participation of all in the church in ministry.

Let me make one additional set of comments before concluding this section and moving to specific suggestions of advocacy. To this point, I have directed attention mainly to the negative connotations (and denotations) of the word "lay." However, when a word is a correlative, or one of a pair, addressing the first has implications for the second. The word "clergy," in Protestantism, is synonymous with "minister" or "ministers," while in Catholicism, the word "priest" is still widely used. In my judgment, the present caste system victimized not only those called "lay," but also those who are ordained, whatever they are called.

> They must attempt to meet the expectations of the system and of the community, while holding on to their personal integrity. Maintaining this balance, while being all things to all men and women, while being heroes, is a most difficult job description. [17]

A change in the language could thus be of benefit to both groups of persons, whether ordained or not, and could lead all in the churches, not only to new models of ministry, but to new modes of participation in ministry as well. How this might be accomplished is the burden of Section III.

III

The following are concrete suggestions offered to those in the church who are seriously engaged in reflection on the work of ministry. Those who have access to pulpit and classroom, to press and publication, and, therefore, to articulation and speech in public forums are most especially involved. However, my hope is that not only they, but all ecclesial persons would give serious consideration to these proposals.

1. *Eliminate the word "lay" from the vocabulary of church language, beginning with the term "lay ministry."*
The most immediate result might indeed be a certain stiltedness and circumlocution. The fact that no other term is readily available is an argument for the urgency of change. A search for more appropriate and equitable terminology is necessary now, before a theology of "lay" ministry is developed. We cannot develop parallel theologies of "lay" ministry and "ordained" ministry: we have to find a single theology of ministry applicable to all. In the past, theologies of service in the church, with the notable exceptions of Congar and Kraemer, have been theologies largely and even exclusively applicable only to the ordained. "Perhaps history is now taking a new turn. What has been on the edges may move toward the center. Such a history would then be written with different views of the church community, and different images of power."[18] Even more important, however, ministry would then begin to be viewed, not as a question of office-bearers arranged with more or less authority, but rather ". . . as service done within and beyond a local community.[19]

2. *Eliminate the word "clergy" from the vocabulary of church language.*
This may be viewed as a move toward "declericalization" but it must be noted that such declericalization cannot be done without the "delaicization" implied in the preceding pages. Ideally, eliminating the term "clergy" cannot be accomplished unless the prior conviction is held that ministry is fundamentally shared by all the baptized. Eliminating "clergy" might have serious consequences but not "if the 'nonclergy' are willing to move up, if the 'clergy' are willing to move over, and if all of God's people are willing to move out"[20] to bear witness to the common enterprise of the gospel.

Realistically, it could even mean a reevaluation of such practices as clerical exemptions from civil service, taxes, and lawsuits and an examination of the reasons behind what appear to be double-standard moral expectations with reference to the ordained. These are especially evident in the sexual area, where they range from refusal to ordain practicing homosexuals in some churches to the refusal to ordain practicing heterosexuals in others.

At the same time, however, I would advocate keeping the term "ministry" to mean the work of the church as a whole, while examining the term "minister" (without qualifiers "lay" and/or "ordained") in order to see how it is viable. The ancient yet vital terms "priest," "priestly," and "priesthood" may be helpful here, not only from a theological perspective but also from an ecumenical one. Presently, for most Catholics, the "minister" is the Protestant clergyman down the block, whereas for most Protestants, the "priest" is that minister's Catholic counterpart. A more careful attentiveness to the corporate dimensions of priesthood and ministry would be an advantage for both churches. Indeed, each of the terms, minister and priest, might even come to have a much broader application for both communions. As Catholics rethink the meaning of ministry and begin to reclaim this language, Protestants might reexamine and reclaim the positive values of priesthood, especially as it is related to mystery, sacrament, and community. First Peter 2:9 is directed to us all: "You are a chosen race, a royal priesthood, a holy nation, God's own people, that you may declare the wonderful deeds of him who called you out of darkness into his marvelous light."

3. *Name the forms ministry is taking today.*

This begins with the scriptural symbols of the priestly, the prophetic, and the political, but it also extends to the forms of service in the world where people live their daily lives. As points of departure, we might consider the classical forms of teaching (*didache*), prayer/worship (*leiturgia*), community (*koinonia*), advocacy (*kerygma*), and outreach (*diakonia*), while encouraging one another, in community, to discover those other areas in which ministry is alive. "I think it is being true to our New Testament heritage to suggest that the church must accept and create forms of ministry which will help unite us, that is, the community must perceive what ministries respond to its needs for reconciliation with God by proclaiming the message of [the] Christ."[21] A point made here, given the central argument of this essay, is the need for ministry to be *pluri*form and *multi*form, rather than dual in form. Moving in the direction of naming many ministries, we reflect the pluriform Pauline description of the ministries of pastor, apostle, prophet, teacher, helper, and administrator while seeking to be true to the *kairos* (opportune moment) of the twentieth century. "If I could state it as a thesis, I would suggest that the reconciliation of ministries lies in accepting the multiple forms, sometimes even in creating new forms, in response to an understanding of the relationship of ministry to the church and to the person of Jesus [the] Christ."[22]

4. *Examine the nature of ordination, especially from the perspective of its being the precise ritual whereby, at present, clergy become clergy and lay become lay.*

Let us ask: (a) who is eligible? (b) who decides who is eligible? (c) who does the ordaining, that is, who is the ordaining agent? (d) for how long is a person to be ordained? (e) to what work is ordination directed? As a public issue, such examination is long overdue and has been delayed in part because the claims of historical precedent and divine inspiration in raising up candidates have been made with such vigor and the theology of office and orders carefully developed. What has not been addressed with similar attention is that, although one *can* claim history and inspiration, the conclusion does not necessarily follow that such divinely inspired historical development is forever normative. Such questions as the five asked earlier are imperative to a church that claims ministry for all. Still, they have not been universally raised. Perhaps this is because we have no alternate models. Thus our ways of doing things appear obviously appropriate because no other way of putting things has occurred to us. With reference to ordination, however, other possibilites do exist, and alternate scenarios are being proposed, not least of which are these suggestions of Rosemary Reuther:

At best, the processes of selecting and educating an ordained ministry should arise from within the self-educative process of the community itself. With trained and committed teachers, the community should be engaged, first of all, in theological self-reflection on its own mission. Out of this process, especially talented and committed persons develop who are designated by the congregation for more specialized training, to be equipped to become teachers and pastors [editor: and many other roles]. Ministerial education should be based on the education of the adult community. For more specialized training in theological and social skills, congregations might band together to create schools. The designating of a person as an ordained leader of a congregation [editor: and other designations] should then be carried out in such a way as to show that it is the community itself which ordains her or him. [23]

Conclusion

My intention in writing this essay has been to raise, at the very least for myself, issues that seem most important for the future of an integral, ecclesial ministry. In no way do I intend it as an *ad hominem* attack on individuals who have given their lives and their persons to the service of God and other human beings. On the contrary I assume such persons, most of them male, are among those most profoundly aware of the difficulties of church form and as eager as I to encourage a universal ministry.

My own interest, as I have tried to make clear, is with the form, structure, and shape of the church. I hope the reader will at least take the time to entertain the possibility that maybe, just maybe, some of what is suggested here is correct. Receiving a hearing and engaging in conversation on these issues is valuable, I hope, for others, but certainly for me. Beyond this, however, I remain one who hopes that a broader, more inclusive, richer form of church and of ministry may yet be ours; and I remain one who dreams for a different kind of church with neither Jew nor Greek, female nor male, clergy nor lay, but where all may be one in the Christ who will be all in all.

The accomplishment of such a hope and such a dream remains, as many feminists have pointed out, a task of naming and transforming symbol and image at the deepest level. Such naming and transforming are catalysts for the birth of a new reality "in which peoples who have traditionally been excluded and invisible are made central." [24] In the birth of a new and chastened language, new myth, and new symbol, we move toward new form and greater wholeness. By doing this we begin to eliminate those forms, structures, and shapes of church life that have led, in the past, to division and exclusivity. Questioning "lay" ministry may be a way of beginning such a re-creation in the church.

Notes

[1] David N. Power, *Gifts That Differ: Lay Ministries Established and Unestablished* (New York: Pueblo Publishing Co., 1980), p. 159.

[2] Hans Kung, *Why Priests?* (New York: Doubleday & Co., Inc., 1972), p. 42.

[3] *Ibid.*, p. 34.

[4] *Ibid.*, p. 33.

[5] Ben Shahn, *The Shape of Content* (New York: Random House, Inc., 1957), p. 81.

[6] See especially Yves Congar, *Lay People in the Church* (Ramsey, N.J.: Paulist Press, 1959); Hendrik Kraemer, *A Theology of the Laity* (Philadelphia: The Westminster Press, 1959); Stephen C. Neill and Hans-Ruedi Weber, eds., *The Layman in Christian History* (Philadelphia: The Westminster Press, 1963).

[7] Hans-Ruedi Weber, "The Battle Is Not Yet Won," *Laity Exchange* (The Audenshaw Foundation, 1978), p. 2 mimeographed.

[8] See "Motherearth and the Megamachine," *Womanspirit Rising: A Feminist Reader in Religion,* ed. Carol P. Christ and Judith Plaskow (New York: Harper & Row, Publishers, Inc., 1979), pp. 43-52.

[9] Carol P. Christ, *Diving Deep and Surfacing* (Boston: Beacon Press, 1980), p. 26.

[10] Casey Miller and Kate Swift, *Words and Women: New Language in New Times* (New York: Anchor, 1976), p. xiii.

[11] Adrienne Rich, *On Lies, Secrets, and Silences* (New York: W.W. Norton & Co., 1979), pp. 247-248.

[12] Alma Graham, in Miller and Swift, *Words and Women,* p. 32. Graham's formulation originally appeared in a letter to the editor of *The Columbia Forum* (Fall, 1974).

[13] Paulo Freire, *Education for Critical Consciousness*, trans. Myra Ramos (New York: The Seabury Press, 1973). p. 96.

[14] "Christ's Ministry Through His Whole Church and Its Ministers," in *Encounter* (Winter 1964), vol. 25, no. 1, quoted in *Theological Foundations for Ministry,* ed. Ray S. Anderson (Grand Rapids: Wm. B. Eerdmans Publishing Co., 1978), p. 435.

[15] *Ibid.*

[16] William J. Bausch, *The Christian Parish: Whispers of the Risen Christ* (Chicago: Fides Claretian, 1980), p. 110.

[17] Ann Kelley and Anne Walsh, "Ordination: A Questionable Goal for Women," *Women and Orders,* ed. Robert J. Heyer (Ramsey, N.J.: Paulist Press, 1974), p. 70.

[18] Power, *Gifts That Differ,* p. 83.

[19] William R. Burrows, *New Ministries: The Global Context* (Maryknoll, N.Y.: Orbis Books, 1980), p. 69.

[20] Thomas Gillespie, "The Laity in Biblical Perspective," *The New Laity,* ed. Ralph D. Bucy (Waco: Word, Inc., 1978), p. 32.

[21] George W. MacRae, "Ministry and Ministries in the New Testament," *The Living Light* (Summer, 1977), vol. 14, no. 2 p. 179.

[22] *Ibid.*, p. 169.

[23] Rosemary Radford Ruether, *New Woman, New Earth* (New York: The Seabury Press, 1975), p. 81. Used by permission of the publisher.

[24] The Cornwall Collective, *Your Daughters Shall Prophesy: Feminist Alternatives in Theological Education* (New York: The Pilgrim Press, 1980), p. 98.

II.

Ministry of the Laity in Action: Cases That Support the Concept

George Peck, Richard Broholm and Maria Harris all perceive a problem with new clarity and urgency. They acknowledge that the church, as currently structured, is not calling forth or sustaining the ministry of the laity in any adequate fashion. Each speaks of a "reconstructive" agenda that might be undertaken by the church in order to move in a more faithful direction.

Does this mean, then, that the ministry of the laity is on hold, awaiting a change from on high? Not at all. The following section offers a perspective by three members of the laity on their ministries in the secular workplace. Carolyn MacDougall describes the shape of her work within a social service agency and the different ways in which she understands that work as ministry; Alan Holliday discusses the possibilities for ministry within the world of advertising; and Jim Stockard relates the impact of a local commissioning service on his work as a member of a housing authority.

These three stories give evidence that while the institutional church may be in need of major change, the body is alive and active. These laity are wrestling with questions of giftedness, issues of call, the anxieties that accompany ambiguous results, and their needs for education, support, and affirmation. They are reporting from the front lines, testifying about the territory that they inhabit day after day.

Ministry in the Work Setting: A Personal Study

Carolyn MacDougall

In light of all the theological arguments calling for a new understanding of how laity do ministry in the world, this article is an attempt to describe, in as clear a way as possible, my own sense of calling to ministry in my particular setting. The description is highly personalized, influenced by my background, skills, and experiences as well as by the situation in which I am working at the time of this writing. Given that, I would like to set forth what I do that I would call ministry, some of the issues for me in determining "call," and some insights about the nature of ministry for laity.

Since I work in one of the "helping" professions, I am acutely aware of differences between ministry in my work place and the ministry of Christians in other occupations. However, there may well be a tendency to exaggerate these differences. I believe that it is much too simplistic to call all forms of human services a ministry, without regard for the specifics. I think that much of how I approach my call to ministry in the work place is similar to the approach to ministry of people in other occupations.

The Context of My Life and Ministry

As I write, I am at a crossroads in my life and in my work. After ten years of work experience in the human services field, I am considering questions about the meaning of that experience for me, trying to understand my role and my calling. In light of my involvement in human services, I am attempting to grapple with an unknown future in the political context of the 1980s. I am also struggling with inescapable feelings of "should" that often catch up with men and women as they approach their thirties: I *should* be making more money than I am making; I *should* think about marriage and children; I *should* be further along in my career and know what I am going to do. The cultural values and assumptions that I as a single woman am confronting, some conscious, some subconscious, are challenging me to look at myself, my values, and my relationship to the world in much deeper ways than in the past. It is a difficult and exciting time of discovery.

I currently work for a state agency, the Massachusetts Office for Children (OFC). OFC is a unique organization as state agencies go. It does not provide direct services, as most do, but, rather, was set up by the Massachusetts legislature in 1973 to function as a watchdog on how children are served by public and private agencies throughout the state. Its basic premise is that children are a nonvoting constituency whose rights need to be protected through advocacy on their behalf by those who are concerned about children (i.e., citizens, parents, and children's services professionals). Advocacy takes many forms within the Office for Children. It includes the task of licensing day-care and residential facilities for children, a statewide policy and planning unit that works with other government agencies on issues related to providing needed children's services, and a system of forty-two local offices and seven regional offices that do individual case advocacy for children and their parents (Help for Children/Information and Referral). The local offices organize volunteer Councils for Children to advocate for children's needs and services on a local level (community development): All four functions—licensing, policy and planning, help for children, and community development—taken together ensure that any child in need of services in Massachusetts will receive them.

My role in OFC has been to work in the community development unit. From 1978 to 1980, I staffed the South Shore Council for Children. For the past six months I have functioned as a supervisor/coordinator for all community development activities in our region, supervising six staff persons who work with their respective Councils for Children in one of seven regions in the state.

As a state agency, the Office for Children has been under fire recently. The governor and secretary of human services have filed legislation to abolish the agency (a move that failed after six months of legislative debate); they have imposed a hiring freeze on all OFC positions (that still continues); and they recently replaced the director of OFC with someone they judged to be more in line with the administration's thinking about OFC. The resultant insecurity and shifts in management (I have worked under three directors in the past two years due to political appointment issues) have effectively blocked OFC from carrying out its purpose and mission. In addition, the tax-cutting referendum, Proposition 2½, passed in Massachusetts just recently. This creates an enormous amount of anxiety about whether or not any of us will have jobs six months from now. As we approach a new legislative session in Massachusetts, there are signs that the governor and secretary of human services may again try to abolish OFC or at least change significantly the function and purpose of the agency. In addition, there are rumors of broad reorganization within human services that would severely affect many of the services that OFC has consistently fought hard for in the past seven years.

Given this organizational context, it is sometimes amazing that any work gets done for the children whom we are mandated to serve. But, in fact, one of the rewards of working in a setting such as OFC is that staff and volunteers work hard and keep their sights set on the issues facing children rather than become preoccupied with the survival of our agency. The political context of OFC, however, does take its toll on me personally and on the energies I have for ministry.

The Issue of "Call"

In describing in detail some of the aspects of my work, I hope to provide a context for understanding the call to ministry as a multidimensional, ongoing process. Within the sphere of work, I experience a call in at least three different ways. The first concerns the overall direction and use of my talents. For me that call is to be a manager of people and resources, an administrator, an organizer, and a leader. The second way I experience a call has to do with the setting in which I choose to use those talents—for now, the Office for Children—and the specific job that I have within that setting. The third aspect of a call is experienced in the daily and sometimes hourly decisions that are a part of my job. It is this last item—the many duties that one faces in one's daily work—that, once the larger questions of vocation and job description and employer are settled, becomes the focus for the content of one's ministry. Support for ministry by the church needs to address both the larger questions and the smaller but crucial everyday questions that a person confronts in the course of doing ministry.

Within the context of my particular work I can also claim three distinct areas of ministry:

1. the explicit aspects of my job description that complement values I ascribe to as a Christian and that I believe provide a ministry in this world;

2. the choices to use my talents and skills in going beyond what is required in my job to do ministry; and

3. the situations when my job requirements are in direct conflict with what my own sense of ministry is and decisions need to be made about what to do.

Let me now give some specific examples of these three areas of ministry.

Explicit Job Description

I choose to work for OFC because I believe in its mission and particularly in its area-based system of advocacy and help for children. OFC has called to the attention of state government, human services agencies, and citizens the needs of some of the most difficult-to-serve children in the state. It has effectively helped thousands of children and families to receive needed assistance by helping to coordinate services for children, developing and attaining funding for services and educating people about crucial social problems that affect children.

I also believe in the concept of citizen participation in helping the government to deliver aid and in empowering citizens and parents to determine how their tax dollars will be spent in their communities. The choice of working for an organization whose goals and purposes I value is not a new one for me but is, rather, a direct outgrowth of the kind of Christianity that emphasizes working in whatever ways possible to speak to the basic needs of humanity and to further God's kingdom on earth. In the past I have worked for other organizations carrying out similar missions compatible with my Christian values and beliefs.

Within OFC's broad mandate my role and the use of my talents and skills involve a more differentiated aspect of ministry. From my experience as a staff member of the South Shore Council for Children, let me give what I hope will be insightful examples of the specific duties that I would call ministry.

A Ministry of Empowerment

I helped volunteers understand the children's service delivery system so that they could develop, with my assistance, their own sense of goals and priorities for the South Shore Council for Children and help resolve children's needs. I recruited volunteers, trained them, assigned them to duties and responsibilities, and functioned as an effective listener to and broker of their concerns. Citizen volunteers organized information programs and fairs for the community at large on such issues as child abuse and neglect, teenage pregnancy, emergency services for families, rights of special needs (handicapped) children, and the needs of low-income families. My role and ministry in this context was to handle the organizational and administrative functions that allow a volunteer group to work effectively.

A Ministry of Meeting Community Needs

I worked closely with other state and private agencies to develop new programs that were needed to service children. One example was an emergency shelter for teenage runaways and victims of child abuse and neglect. Meeting this need involved advocating for funds from state and federal agencies and identifying a social service agency willing to provide the emergency home in a community-based setting. This shelter, after almost four years of complex negotiations and advocacy, is about to open on the South Shore.

Another example of program development is the work I put

into ensuring that long-term administrative responsiblity was assumed for a program in Quincy providing social services, education, parenting skills, and child care for teenage mothers and their children. (The South Shore Council had initiated the program, and I wanted to ensure its continuity while at the same time letting go of any direct involvement).

A final example of ministry to children on the South Shore was my involvement in paving the way for agencies to coordinate their resources to provide comprehensive emergency services to families and children in crises on a twenty-four hour, seven-days-a-week basis. A basic principle of this service was to support children within the context of their family environment as much as possible.

A Ministry of Advocacy for the Weak and Vulnerable

I worked for advocacy within the state system to ensure that the services delivered to children and families were of good quality. One such example was my involvement in creating a coalition of human service providers and citizens to monitor the delivery of services to abused and neglected children. When, in 1979, two hundred reported cases of suspected child abuse and neglect in the Quincy area were discovered to be unassigned, we provided information to the children's service community on how to help these overlooked families. At the same time we pressed the agency directly responsible for handling child abuse cases to hire more qualified social workers in order to alleviate the number of uncovered cases and relieve stressful working conditions facing its social work staff. Another example was my involvement in training volunteers to review and make recommendations on the state's funding of day-care centers, all the while keeping in mind the need for quality day care at a reasonable cost.

A Ministry of Caring and Evoking the Ministry of Others

Presently as regional coordinator for OFC, I have had different responsibilities, most of which complement and support similar kinds of activities throughout the whole region rather than just in one area. Beyond the use of my organizational, planning, and administrative skills, which lie behind the examples I have listed thus far, I am now specially responsible for the growth and development of the individuals that I supervise. It is a challenge to supervise staff and volunteers and a real joy to know that because I provide encouragement, motivation, and criticism, someone has learned something invaluable about himself or herself. One person, for example, had trouble setting limits on her time and saying no to the many demands placed on her as a community organizer working with volunteers. I have worked with her on her assertiveness skills and helped her to understand the necessity for her to respect herself, both as a person who has a family and a life of her own outside of work, and as an organizer who must sometimes let go and allow volunteers to take more complete responsibility for the projects they initiate. A more difficult ministry for me is giving feedback to people who are not doing their jobs well and helping them to identify realistic goals for improvement or, in a caring way, to see that their skills are not appropriate for the job.

Beyond the Job Description

The second area of ministry involves a desire and an ability to give more to the Office for Children and to the people within it than is necessary to do an adequate job.

A Ministry of Caring

In my interaction with members of the staff as a supervisor, I am perceived by many of them as a source of support for issues they are struggling with in their personal lives. Many times, during my supervision, conversation moves from work issues to deeply personal concerns, and I need to decide whether to direct our talk back to work or to allow the person to share what is important at the time. The ministry in these situations is to create an atmosphere of trust, to listen actively, and to care about the whole person, not just the "9-to-5" person. Sometimes I simply listen; other times I share my own experiences. Sometimes I offer help in very pragmatic ways, and other times I refer a staff person to people or resources that can help in a way that I can't.

A Ministry of Organizational Leadership

As community representative and as regional coordinator, I choose to help solve some of the longstanding organizational problems that have existed within OFC. I simply will not allow past history and numerous excuses for why problems have not been dealt with before to prevent me from attempting to address them now. Thus, I was labeled a "rabble rouser" by our former director for articulating statewide the needs of all community representatives for more support from our central office. "Rabble rouser" was an affectionate label, and in fact the director began to address some of the concerns before he left the agency. As regional coordinator I became quickly frustrated with the difficulties our central office was facing in peforming its functions, partly because of its shortage of staff and partly because of external pressures it weathered. I convinced the other six regional coordinators that we could work together on projects of concern to us and to our staff statewide and that our monthly meetings could include much more dialogue and cross-fertilization of ideas than was happening at the time.

In Conflict with the Job

The third area, those times when work and what I think my ministry should be contradict each other, is the most difficult to describe. Some examples of issues I deal with may help to give a picture of this area.

Recommendation Differences

Office for Children is, by design, a participatory structure. The legislature in creating OFC clearly intended to require citizen participation in how tax dollars are spent on children's services within their communities. This participation is done via Council for Children committees that review proposals for children's services and make recommendations to funding agencies on those proposals. As an OFC staff person, my role is to support and advocate for the positions that the councils take on these proposals.

I believe in this process for two reasons: (1) the process empowers the citizens involved, giving them the tools and training to make an impact on decisions that affect their lives and their children's lives; and (2) it has been shown again and again that citizens are more concerned about quality of care, about whether or not a funded program meets a real community need, and about the effective use of their tax dollars for children's services than are the state agencies involved in funding. Citizens are also more immune to political and other pressures that are often the unstated reasons for agency funding of programs. Translated into Christian values, supporting citizen participation is a ministry of empowerment, stewardship, and protection of the weak and vulnerable (children).

Sometimes, however, citizens make recommendations that I personally believe are wrong and are not the best for the children being served. The conflict usually has to do with quality of care or with a major factor the citizens overlook, such as budget realities or relative need. In these situations I can sometimes handle the conflict in negotiation with the citizen group and the state agency and reach a compromise satisfactory to all. But sometimes I will advocate the citizen position despite my personal opinion, in the belief that 90 percent of the time citizen recommendations are as sound, if not more so, as what the agency had decided in the past. I will go 100 percent for citizen participation and accept the fact that 10 percent of the time their recommendations are wrong.

Accountability Differences

Another example of conflict arises from the unsure reality of working for OFC under the current administration. I have two bosses: the Council for Children, composed of volunteers, and the director of OFC, who is accountable for her job and her staff to the secretary of human services and the governor. There are times when the Councils for Children take stands that are directly in opposition to those of the secretary and the governor, particularly when it comes to legislation. Two examples this past year were the governor's legislation to abolish OFC (which the councils opposed) and the councils' support of a cost-of-living increase to recipients of Aid to Families with Dependent Children (which the governor opposed).

In the past, Community Development staff have been allowed to work on and provide OFC with resources (paper, printing, postage) for any position on children's issues that the councils have formally voted to support or oppose. This

year the secretary has intimated that staff time and the resources of OFC cannot be spent on supporting any council
position counter to that of the administration. It is unclear
whether or not that policy will be carried out, but if it is, it will
severely limit my ability to assist the councils' speaking out
on significant issues of child welfare.

The Gray Areas

There are a number of gray areas in children's services, and
from time to time in OFC a "hot" issue will emerge in relation
to which there is no single "morally just" course of action. For
instance, any evaluation of a program done by OFC or a
council will have consequences. If a council report on the
quality of a program that serves children raises serious questions about that program's adequacy, consequences as far-
reaching as forcing a program to close its doors are possible.
If there are no alternative programs in the immediate area,
then service can be disrupted for the children and their families for an indefinite period, and in some cases severe problems can result that are worse than the original issue of the
program's quality. Sometimes the children's receiving contin-
uous care is more important than the question of quality.
Other times the issue of no alternatives becomes a scapegoat
for continuing to support poor quality programs, and a period
of disruption in order to develop a new program is the only
way to achieve a "greater good" later on. I try, in working with
staff and council members, to find the best course of action
given the circumstances; but sometimes there is no good
choice.

As I write this, the largest residential care provider for adolescents in the state is having a board meeting to decide
whether or not it will close. It operates a system of group
homes that serves 1500 adolescents with $5.2 million worth
of contracts from state agencies. Several of the main factors
in their decision making are the decision of two state agencies
to stop funding some of their programs, the fiscal difficulties
the agencies face because of the way the state pays its con-
tracted vendors, and a licensing report written by the former
OFC director that documents numerous violations of mini-
mum standard of care. That report has not been made official

yet but was "leaked" to a number of people, including the press.

While I am personally glad that the concerns of several councils and OFC about these programs are finally being addressed, it is disturbing to think about 1500 adolescents who are in need of group residential care being turned out into the streets, back to possible destructive home environments, or into other inappropriate settings that may do more damage than good.

It is unclear, at this writing, how the issue will be resolved or what role, if any, I will play in it. But if I were to play a role, it could well conflict with the objectives of my job description, at least in the short run.

New Directions, New Questions of Calling

By describing the details of my work at the Office for Children and some of the complexities involved in attempting to do ministry within that setting, it is my hope that the ambiguities I have experienced are helpful not only to those in traditional "helping" professions but also to those within other work settings.

It seems that many factors enter into one's decisions about work, including much that is beyond an individual's control to plan or to change. One of the more challenging aspects of working for OFC and, I suspect, for all of state government in the wake of Proposition 2½, is that change occurs very quickly and rumors abound. The legislative budget process, which determines the fate of most state agencies, occurred after the original draft of this essay, and for several months rumors floated and actual threats were made concerning whether or not the agency would survive. It has survived, in fact, but not without severe pain, layoffs, the loss of another director, and a reduction in services. Office for Children has hardly been alone this year as a target of budget cuts, and the larger picture of the future of government funding for human services in Massachusetts and in the nation has become dismal at best.

During the fall and winter of 1980-81, I made a decision to pursue a master's degree in business administration. After much support and affirmation from a variety of sources, I definitely feel called to leadership and managerial roles. The decision to pursue an M.B.A. is based partly on a desire to increase my technical knowledge of management principles and practice and partly on a reaction to the uncertainty as to what shape government or human services will take in the next decade. At this time in my life I am anxious to test out new career possibilities, including opportunities within the private business sector. At the same time, I have chosen an M.B.A. program in which a substantial part of my course work is oriented toward public and nonprofit management. I am currently a full-time M.B.A. candidate at Boston University.

Being a student again refocuses for me the question of ministry. At the beginning of this essay I contended that, for most people, the content of ministry consists of coping with the particulars of a job description and work setting, the daily decisions to do or not to do ministry, and the conflicts those decisions can create. For me, however, there are now new issues of call: What skills do I develop? What settings shall I work in, in the future? During the last four months, those questions have arisen weekly, as I have been exposed to many more possibilities than I could have imagined myself considering previously.

The Need for Support

During the past year I have participated in a small group comprised of members of the Church of the Covenant in Boston. We have met weekly to explore our ministries in our varied work settings and to provide support to one another in identifying and affirming directions to take that are appropriate to our skills, interest, and values. While the focus has been primarily on work, more personal issues in the lives of group members have surfaced as well. Usually the group meetings open and close with prayer and provide opportunity for each person to share a current or ongoing concern. Members provide feedback—often challenging, affirming, or reflective in nature—to help one another sort through, within a Christian frame of reference, feelings and thoughts. Occasionally, particularly when a member is facing major decisions regarding his or her work future, the group will devote the entire two hours to helping that person focus on his or her talents and the options and possibilities that exist. Essential ingredients of such a support group are the development of a high level of trust, agreement on a particular method of facilitation, members who are willing and able to be supportive and active listeners, and a sense of continuity achieved through frequent, regularly scheduled meetings and a commitment by members to meet together over a period of time.

For me, this group has provided an important place in which to reflect on the daily and long-range concerns of my life and work. The group has helped me face the almost constant turmoil at Office for Children; it has supported me in my decision to return to school by helping me to decide which schools to apply to and by suffering with me through the questions, doubts, and anxiety of waiting to be accepted. And, when acceptance and a scholarship award made the "dream" of attending school full time a reality, the group celebrated with me as well. The opportunity to listen to and support other people in their concerns has been helpful as well. I have come to recognize that many of the issues and conflicts that I face are not unique but are quite similar to those of other Christians wishing to integrate their religious values with their daily existence. The insight gained from being a supportive listener has thus been invaluable for me.

Finally, participation in this support group has provided for me an important sense of connectedness with the wider community of people who belong to Church of the Covenant. It has allowed me, as a new person to the church, to get to know people on a more intimate basis and has increased my desire to be an involved member of the church community.

It is my expectation that the support group will continue to be a source of affirmation and challenge as I face new questions resulting from being in school. I expect that the members will continue to call me to accountability as a Christian and help me to define my particular calling as I explore various options. I know that they will pray with me, ask tough questions, listen reflectively, and provide insights.

What has arisen for me from this experience is the new consciousness I have in asking the question "What is my ministry in this situation?" In the future, depending upon what happens in the next two years, I may not be able to describe my ministry in the work setting as easily or with as much clarity as I have been able to do at Office for Children. But I am convinced that as I enter new situations, I will discover, with the support of other Christians, many new possibilities for ministry, whether they be within a work setting, within my community, with family or friends, or a combination of settings.

Discovering a Ministry Where One Ought Not to Exist

Alan Holliday

Before reflecting on a kind of ministry in the work place, I'd like to note my starting point. It is ten before seven on a Tuesday evening and I've been home for half an hour. My wife and I have yet to eat because our children are off at various activities; so I've taken the time to recall just what comprised my business day.

I am a copy writer. I write advertisements for a large Boston agency. My major client, for whom I worked exclusively this day, is a sizable New England bank and financial holding company. To aid its marketing efforts, I wrote copy for a sign that will appear in the windows of its branch offices announcing a contest for customers. The winner, after using an automatic teller machine once a week for the next six weeks, will receive a small, but very usable sailboat. I wrote copy for a similar sign for the contest that will be placed elsewhere in the bank. I discussed production of a campaign of our TV commercials for a new savings product that the bank will soon offer. And I outlined a newspaper ad announcing the bank's financial performance for the first half of the year.

I am well paid to do these things. I try to be conscientious in my work. However, I consider much of it frivolous and find it hard to imagine any of it as ministry.

Perhaps a closer look at one part of the day I outlined will explain my feelings. A good example is the ad I worked on, which details the bank's earnings record. Of course, the record was impressive. People don't consciously put their names on ads that reflect a poor image. Indeed, the bank's performance was so outstanding that it wants various people to know its record. Some will purchase the stock. Others will find security in dealing with a successful bank. For these reasons and because employees, current shareholders, and officers can all feel proud, the ad will appear. It will appear at no small expense, and there's little on earth to prevent it. What's more, I'll write it. I'll be a party to a relatively unproductive, yet rather costly endeavor.

Some could rightly ask, "What's his problem? He's already admitted to being well paid." Others might note that what I do is part of the American economic system and, therefore, contains little inherent wrong. What's more, I enjoy what I do and the interesting, bright people with whom I work. An associate of mine once said he loves doing advertising, "Because of all the business people out there, we're the ones who get to dance in the end zone." Advertising is the glamorous side of business. The artist and writers are stars of a sort, and it's nice to be a star. It's fun seeing your work on television and in magazines and newspapers. On a superficial level, I can't imagine doing anything that's more enjoyable or personally rewarding.

There is, however, a dark side of advertising, and countless critics have recognized it. The late Howard Gossage, who enjoyed a successful career in the field, perhaps spoke for many in one soul-searching remark. "Advertising expresses a power relationship," Gossage observed. "One person, the advertiser, invades; millions absorb. And to what end? So that people will buy something! A deep, profound and disturbing act by the few against the many for a trivial purpose."[1]

Variations on this negative view are often heard and with some justification. On the other hand, in a capitalistic society, advertising can help to stimulate the economy, bring useful products to the market and benefits to many. I should also mention that advertising has been put to obvious good use in promoting conservation and public safety, in soliciting funds for charitable organizations, and even in encouraging church attendance. Many of these efforts are donated by advertising firms.

So, as in many businesses, there is good and bad in what

I do. It remains for the lay minister to bring about a greater amount of good.

A Ministry of Imagination

Perhaps because my work generally involves imagination, I consider imagination a valuable tool in pursuit of a lay ministry. For instance, someone in my position could consider the assignment to do the bank's earnings announcement as a golden opportunity (if you'll excuse the use of that expression here). What might happen, for instance, if the bank ran a smaller ad than the full page it had planned? It could still tell its earnings story, be proud of that, and possibly give the extra money from advertising to charity. This is not likely, but there's always the hope. Even if it kept the funds and invested them in employee benefits, that action would represent a significant step forward. So one recommends taking that course.

If this sounds utopian, it is, to a large extent. I've tried it though; it sometimes works, and I don't intend to let up. I might also point out that others in my position could attempt to do the same. Corporate advertising managers should try it. Senior executives ought to get in on the fun. It's merely a matter of asking "Why am I doing things this way? Could I discharge my duties to the people who employ me and to my clients and yet attempt to create some far-reaching good?" Merely the act of considering it is enjoyable, challenging, and sound Christian thinking.

A number of people have told me that they wake up in the middle of the night with a smashing idea. I've often done that, too. It's something about the subconscious, I suppose, but it leads to a further suggestion. Why not give odd moments of thinking time to a review of your work place and how it could be changed to benefit others? There are product, pricing, and personnel opportunities. Any number of problems could use an inventive Christian approach. You don't have to write ads or control budgets to have creative ideas. German theologian Dorothee Soelle encourages inventive thinking to reach Christian goals in today's society. She recommends the virtues of "tolerance and humor, righteous anger and empathy, initiative and the cultivation of a productive power of imagination."[2]

I am fortunate to work in an environment that permits and encourages these qualities. The typical advertising agency is a blend of business people, both in sales and finance, matched with a nearly equal number of artists and writers. This makes for a high degree of tolerance of one's fellow workers and permits a diversity of opinions to exist. If my ideas are interesting, creative, and sensible from a business standpoint, they will be heard. The fact that they stem from Christian beliefs is of little concern to my associates, although they realize that this may often be the case. What I'd like to stress, just as Dr. Soelle has, is the opportunity for the creative expression of Christianity. I am convinced that this blend of initiative and imagination has its place throughout the business world and that every Christian is called upon to exercise these faculties. I need hardly remind you that Jesus issued his call to all who work—fishermen, tax collectors, and tent makers.

The best advertising flows from a good basic idea and not the words and pictures that are quite often seen as "creative." The idea comes from thorough knowledge of the product and the marketplace. It seems only logical that those in any particular business environment would be best able to come up with the creative thinking that could change it.

Here it is my duty also to issue a warning. I lost one job because of my involvement with Christian ideals. After a management change in a former agency, my views were no longer met with a great deal of enthusiasm. While this lack of reception was disappointing, it also provided an illuminating experience. In a recession and at a time when few writers of my age have a job, I received several unsolicited offers. The point, I believe, is if you're good at your work and willing to work hard, people will welcome both you and your Christian viewpoint.

A Ministry of Learning

I have shared my time at work, but this is only a portion of my entire day. I've recently completed a second year of part-time study at a nearby divinity school. I don't plan to be any more of a minister than I am right now. The decision to attend classes stemmed from my ignorance and curiosity concerning religious topics. I also felt a need to clarify my own theology. It's interesting, I think, that more and more people are pursuing formal theological training—people who don't plan to be ordained but who choose to do secular work.

I attend classes with the understanding of my employer. I accept less salary for the periods when I go and more when I work full-time. I won't dwell on the experience except to say that I've had some wonderful, sometimes frustrating, and often exciting times. I've been exposed to people and ideas that I wouldn't ordinarily have encountered. This is just another way of saying that others might benefit from a real exploration of their faith, i.e., an academic approach to the Bible, theology, and many areas of applied theology. The going is rough at times; at other times it's amazingly clear; but what it all boils down to is thinking deeply about God's message, how one should interpret it, and how one should put it to use. It is, in a way, the whole armor of God that Paul urged we put on.

It isn't necessary to attend theological school to obtain this knowledge. If, however, a school is nearby, it's worth investigating any courses that might fit into a working schedule. If a seminary isn't nearby, there is a large number of clergy who would be more than pleased to share their learning, their personal libraries and their enthusiasm. One need not be limited by denomination; the minister of another denomination down the street is worth knowing, as well as your own minister. One of the best bits of education I picked up was from a Maryknoll priest. A friend of mine visits a local rabbi from time to time and has encountered a wealth of Old Testament understanding.

One of my favorite thoughts was expressed by William E. Diehl, a layman active in church affairs and a successful executive. He recognized the dichotomy between the outlooks of clergy and business leaders. "The preacher starts with the theology and then works it into examples of real-life situations. The layperson starts with the real-life situation and then has a need for the theology which applies to it. The difference is crucial."[3] Diehl goes on to note the difficulties that clergy face in grasping the many kinds of problems that occur in the work place. Usually, the prospective minister has had scant opportunity to study what goes on there. The opportunity dwindles once this person goes into parish work. Therefore, I believe an educated laity is something of a necessity if a laity-clergy dialog is to exist and bring about greater change. For these reasons, I urge a ministry of learning for many and an appreciation of that ministry for everyone.

A Ministry of Presence

I suppose in most work situations people are aware of others with strong religious beliefs. Sometimes the latter are thought of as odd; at other times they're simply tolerated. Occasionally, they're valued. Because of the Bible I keep on my office bookshelf and the theology classes I attend from time to time, there is little doubt as to where my outside interests lie. Curiously enough, people seem interested in what I'm about. Perhaps it was similar for Jesus and his disciples who drew inquiring audiences in their travels.

People drop in to chat about my schooling. At times they come by with problems. I don't pretend to offer much more than a sympathetic ear and understanding, but perhaps these things are most needed in a business environment. I'm aware of the many tensions that our work produces and am familiar with some of the personalities involved. I try to offer support and perhaps direction to those who visit me. I don't set up shop as a minister. No business would permit it. Companies do, however, welcome individuals who can aid others. I try to provide this aid in some small way.

The preacher mentioned in the earlier quote by William Diehl can only hope to hear about the business of preparing ads, shipping an order of computers across the country, negotiating a difficult contract, or whatever people do for a living. The Christian lay minister deals with those problems every day. Who is better able to offer the aid and comfort of Christ to fellow workers?

I once heard of a man who attempted this service of aid by calling others into his office and offering to pray with them. Those in his department began to avoid him and dread the times when he was around. I am suggesting that people need only be available to offer a Christian presence—one that asks to be led by the Lord, to do and say the right and comforting thing.

Postscript

Few who read these words will find themselves in just my situation, but practically everyone experiences times when work is not as fully satisfying as it might be or is in conflict with Christian beliefs.

I would like to think that those are the very moments when Christ is sustaining us the most and calling on us to stay at our work. If we are to bring the ideals of Jesus to this world, the initiative may originate in the sanctuary, but it will have its realization in the offices and on the production lines of our country's businesses.

Notes

[1] Jerry Mander, *Four Arguments for the Elimination of Television* (New York: Morrow Quill Paperbacks, 1978), p. 17.

[2] Dorothee Soelle, *Beyond Mere Obedience*, trans. Lawrence W. Denef (New York: The Pilgrim Press, 1982), p. 63.

[3] William E. Diehl, *Christianity and Real Life* (Philadelphia: Fortress Press, 1976), p. 34.

Commissioning the Ministries of the Laity: How It Works and Why It Isn't Being Done

Jim Stockard

For nearly forty years, Sunday church school teachers, leading laity and denominational leaders have been saying to me "Make your faith a seven-day-a-week way of life." But I first heard those words in a life-changing way six years ago. They were spoken to me by a fellow member of the laity, in the midst of a worship service in our own church community. My own work was being lifted up in a special ceremony. In the space of this ten-minute celebration, I felt more challenged and supported than I ever had by any eloquent sermon, forceful Sunday church school lesson, or dynamic author. My own ministry was affirmed and the concept of the ministry of the laity was affirmed as well.

That ceremony, known as "commissioning" in our church, has nourished me over the years. I return to it periodically, read over the words, even discuss specifics with members of the congregation. Others in our community who have been commissioned tell me that their experiences have been the same. The purpose of this essay is to analyze why these commissionings have been important to me and to others, and why, sadly, they are almost impossible to perform in many churches today.

Five Important Aspects of the Commissioning Process

Let us take a close look at what is involved in a commissioning.

The Commissioning Is Based in the Whole Congregation

Several people work on writing each commissioning, and several more speak during the ceremony. The entire congregation confirms the challenge and promises support. Thus, the whole community is concentrated on one person and his or her ministry. This focus, in turn, helps that person to clarify the core of his or her ministry, its opportunities, and its direction. For me, the resulting feelings were not unlike those I suspect David must have had as he went out to face the giant.

The power of having a community behind you is demonstrated by the story of Julia, a woman in our congregation who has not been commissioned but who has appropriated for herself the same kinds of affirmation from our community for her work as a school teacher. Several years ago there was a controversy in our city over whether the superintendent of schools should be dismissed or retained. He was a rigid, harsh, and, to my mind, racist individual. The city was split over the issue, as was the school committee. When the teachers' union came to vote on the matter, the superintendent put heavy pressure on the members to support him. The discussion was intense, and Julia spoke eloquently against his reappointment, but when the vote came in, it was 199 to 6, with Julia one of the six against reappointment. Later when I asked Julia how she found the courage to speak and vote like that, she said, "I knew it was what anybody at Old Cambridge Baptist Church would have done and would have wanted me to do. So it was easy."

Commissioning Is Part of a Public Worship Service

Because of the centrality of worship in our congregation's life and because of our desire to link our worshiping lives with our vocational lives, it has always been important to us that these commissioning ceremonies be part of our Sunday morning services. We do not relegate them to a special time or isolate them in a separate ceremony. Rather, we put them at the center of our corporate lives.

The public nature of the ceremony is important for the person being commissioned, for the congregation, and for newcomers to the community. For the commissioned person the gathering is a source of power and support. For the congregation, the reciting of the commissioning informs us and stimulates our concern about one another's work. In spite of our commitment to mutual support, we still know very little about one another's working lives. The commissioning helps correct this deficiency and provides information that can form the basis for contacts, conversations, or prayers.

For visitors or newcomers the commissioning makes clear that we take seriously the dimension of our working lives. It may also be an occasion for them to begin reflecting on their own ministries.

The Commissioning Is Always a Two-Way Street

The specifics of each service are broken into three parts. According to the particulars of the situation, the congregation says:

—Here is the situation you face.

—Here is what we expect from you in this situation.

—Here is what we will do to support you.

We see this as a responsible way of dealing with one another in terms of the realities of our society. We also hear in it echoes of our biblical heritage. God frequently spoke to the Israelites in exactly these terms:

—Here is what you must face.

—Here is what I require of you.

—Here is how I will help you through this trial.

The commissioning service also testifies to our interdependence. In the face of individual and social problems, we are besieged with one-dimensional solutions. At one extreme we are counseled to be totally self-reliant, to believe in a modern form of rugged individualism which promises that if only we set our minds and bodies to it, we can do anything we want. At the other extreme, we hear philosophies that urge us to let go, to let government or God take on all of our problems. Our commissioning services take a middle path. We say that individual responsibility is critical for bringing in the kingdom of God. But we also insist that little progress is possible without the ongoing support of a community.

Commissions Are Theologically Grounded

That which distinguishes our commissions from actions that a college alumni group or a democratic ward committee might perform is their theological grounding. The ultimate authority on which we draw is that of the Great Commission (Matthew 28:19-20). We are not able to say to one another, "We will be with you always," but we are able to say, "God will be with you always." And we are bold enough to say, "What that means is that you will not be alone in your ministry. For the present we are your support community; we will be there with you. In the future it may be someone else." With biblical and theological truths we attempt both to challenge and to reassure the commissioned person.

The Commissionings Are Specific

The services are not platitudes or general affirmations of our commitment to the Golden Rule. They are as concrete as we can make them. When I was commissioned to my ministry as a member of the Cambridge Housing Authority Board of Commissioners, the words of my service referred to a bankrupt, insensitive public agency, plagued by nepotism and vacant units, and alienated from the residents. I was asked to involve residents and the broader community in solving agency problems, to open up vacant units, to work against racism, to bring in expert staff, and to speak out on issues that could not be solved from within the agency. The church pledged to write letters to the agency and to the media, to come to public meetings if I asked, and to provide financial help for me and my family if my activities should cause problems for the consulting firm with which I work.

In order to be this specific, several people from the congregation had to learn a great deal about what lay before me. Their knowledge challenges me to perform because I know that others know about my work and will be wanting to know what progress is being made. Those persons are also more ready to respond when I need help. Several times, when faced with thorny problems, I have asked half a dozen members of the congregation to meet with me. Each time I have come away with new ideas and with new strength. This degree of support would not be possible if we dealt with one another at the level of abstractions.

Why then, with all the conspicuous benefits of the commissioning process, haven't more churches undertaken similar rituals? I can witness to the potency of this process. I feel truly called to a ministry with the Cambridge Housing Authority. (Interestingly, while I define my vocational work as a housing consultant for low income groups as being equally a ministry, I do not have the same sense of calling and purpose with that responsiblity as I have with the Housing Authority. While there are other differences, I have been commissioned for my work with the latter, but not with the former.)

Five Blocks to Commissioning

I know of no member of the laity or ordained minister who would not want the same sense of calling and commitment for every member of his or her congregation. Yet this kind of commissioning process is still rare. Let me suggest five possible roadblocks to the widespread use of commissionings in our churches.

The Jealousy of Clergy Relating to Their Own Special Status

The block that I have encountered most often is the desire of clergy to preserve the "set-apartness" of their role in God's world.

I have heard pastors say that ordination is the church's equivalent of passing the bar for lawyers or licensure for doctors. But when I then suggest that they need commissionings just as their parishioners do, they indicate that they have already been commissioned in their ordination. When I suggest that we ordain all members, they balk. I have heard pastors suggest that all Christians are ordained through baptism. When I then ask why they need a second ordination if the rest of us don't, there is no answer. It seems to be an inbred belief among clergy that ordination is something unique for a chosen few.

I sense that this feeling on their part strikes at the heart of their ability to encourage and affirm other ministries within the institutional structures. Ordination is the church's supreme (and, in many cases, only) rite for the recognizing of gifts. If it is reserved for clergy, then clearly my lay gifts and ministry must be secondary. In fact, they probably don't matter very much because the kingdom will arrive through the work of the clergy, right? I mean, it's nice to be a competent amateur and all that, but you can't really expect me to take on any big responsibilities for God's work here, can you?

I suspect that it was partly this kind of thinking that allowed the officially proclaimed leading member of the laity of the church in which I grew up to be a violent racist. Had our pastor been able to convey to him that they shared *equally* the responsibility for God's work in that place, the man might have reconsidered some of his words and actions.

God has given us each gifts—some for preaching, some for teaching, some for prophesying—and surely some for managing, some for parenting, some for counseling, some for entertaining. Until clergy can enthusiastically relinquish their "more equal" status among God's people, I see little possibility for calling forth the ministries of the whole people of God.

Our Lack of Knowledge About What Each Other Does with His or Her Life

At Old Cambridge Baptist Church, which I consider the closest religious community to which I have belonged and one of the closest of which I have read, I am troubled to say that there are only a few people whose work and ministry I really know about. For most I know a title—"teacher," "lawyer," "political activist," "parent." For some I know enough to describe the tasks they perform daily and the kinds of people with whom they work. For only a handful could I name the critical human and spiritual issues with which they are currently wrestling.

I am not naive enough to believe that I can know the details of all of the ministries in our congregation. But I do sense that I could know more than I do, and I sense that there are some persons in our community whose ministries are not known to anybody (including possibly themselves). If we want to support the ministries of one another in life-changing ways, a first step seems to be to know what those ministries are.

Our Unwillingness to Get Close Enough to One Another to Truly Challenge and Support One Another in Our Ministries

After knowledge comes some level of intimacy. There are very few people at Old Cambridge Baptist Church (my wife and four or five others) whom I feel free to call and ask for time and for help. I call on them when I am stuck, when I face a critical problem I don't know how to solve, when my own resources and those of prayer aren't enough. I call on those others and ask them to act on their commitment to me so that I can act on mine to them. In these sessions, sometimes one-on-one, sometimes in a small group, all the barriers come down. I don't have to speak as a "public official" or a "professional" in the housing field or a "liberal." Nor do my friends need to play any of their normal roles. We are people struggling jointly with problems that beset some of God's people—in this case, poor, often troubled families, living in an unsafe and degrading housing complex. And we are under a Great Commission to do something about it, using what gifts each of us has.

These sessions of conversation are of enormous help to me. They are also deep and searching and intimate. They are the critical follow-up to the public commissionings. Without the ongoing support, the formal celebration means little. I fear that the hard work necessary to pave the way for this level of involvement with each other as persons and as ministers will be resisted in many quarters. It is not easy in this era of self-actualization to take a stand saying, "I need to give help, and I need to receive it." But I think it is important to move in that direction.

Our Tendency to Judge Between Those Callings That Are Ministries and Those That Are Not

Doctors and nurses can be viewed as ministers. Stock brokers cannot be. Social workers and many teachers qualify. Corporate executives do not. Civil rights lawyers are doing God's work, but divorce lawyers are not. Liberal Democrats are okay; Republicans are suspect. And parenting and befriending aren't even on the list.

Distinctions like these have been prominent in my experience with the church. Even when the words say otherwise or remain unspoken, the judgments are still being made. And as long as this first class/second class hierarchy exists, it will be very difficult for us to commission all of the ministries that are present in our congregations.

The existence of the divisions creates a twofold problem. First, it's hard for us to work up the commitment and enthusiasm for commissioning some other person if we know or suspect that our own activities won't receive that same attention.

Second, and perhaps more damaging, it is difficult to claim our own work as ministry if it falls into one of the "unblessed" categories. If we can't recognize the ways in which our own work can serve God, it's hard to see how the rest of the church can recognize it. By not recognizing our work as ministry, we slip into the habit of separating our Sunday church life from the remainder of our lives.

I think these problems point to a fundamental failure of theological vocabulary and thinking. We haven't learned how to describe the stockbroker's work in terms of ministry. Consequently a Christian stockbroker doesn't know how to decide if she or he is carrying out a ministry or not. Our tendency in this area has been to adopt technical measures—if you're a stockbroker and a Christian you should be good at what you do. Good Christian stockbrokers are ones who make the most money for their clients. Or we adopt soft, "churchy" standards: it doesn't matter how much money you make for people as long as you treat them nicely.

What if we applied the two Great Commandments to the work of a stockbroker? What does it mean for a stockbroker to love God with all his or her heart, mind, and soul and to love a neighbor as oneself? I think that's a hard question. But I'll bet most churchgoing stockbrokers haven't been asked to grapple seriously with it. And what question could be more important for the church to pose to the stockbroker? Maybe it takes a year of questioning and testing and tentative answers to arrive at a statement of what ministry means in this profession. Maybe it takes five years. Maybe it takes a lifetime. But isn't it the church's role to initiate the process of questioning?

Our Reluctance to Commission Everybody

At Old Cambridge Baptist Church we have commissioned a dozen people. They have tended to be those whose work was most public and most easily identifiable as ministry. That is probably a good starting place. Those cases have a clarity that makes them models for others who are trying to find ministry in their own work.

But I do not think that we have gone far enough. As surely as God has given gifts to all of the children, so should the church help all people to find their gifts and to use them in a ministry that they and the church can celebrate. There will be those who have a difficult time identifying their gifts and their calling. These are the people with whom the church will have to work hardest. But my sense is that we will not have been entirely fruitful until we have commissioned *every member* in our congregation, some perhaps several times.

Finally, let me suggest that *bringing in the kingdom* is the ministry of all God's people. God gives no gifts without a purpose. If our churches are to carry out their mission, a large part of their work must be the uncovering and celebrating of those gifts and the commissioning of the ministries in which the gifts are employed. That process requires hard work, boldness, centeredness, and humility. But these qualities, too, are some of the gifts that God has given us. Finding ourselves so equipped, let us press on toward the goal.

III.

Grappling with the Theological Issues

N ow that we have seen the world from the weekday perspective, let us look at the implications of lay ministry from the standpoint of the Christian tradition. The following three papers explore the ministry of the laity in its theological context.

Carolyn MacDougall and Jim Stockard have raised questions about the call to ministry and to whom it comes. George Peck approaches the question of who is called by way of a survey of biblical literature. He differs from Jim Stockard in postulating that there is a general call to all and a more specific call to ministry, which comes to only a few—or to which only a few respond. He sets forth criteria for judging this call and suggests the need for new structures to legitimize the calls to laity that carry them into the secular work place.

Questions surrounding the appropriate role of the ordained were implied by Jim Stockard and Alan Holliday. M. B. Handspicker here reviews the New Testament from the vantage point of church order and concludes that teaching ought to constitute the center of clerical identity, while liturgical leadership should be opened to the entire community in order to enhance laity's sense of itself as a "royal priesthood."

The relationship between the ministries of the ordained and those of the laity are now addressed by Gabriel Fackre, who describes their complementarity in terms of "identity" and "vitality." He also examines further the territory that Carolyn MacDougall opened, looking at the content of the ministry of the body of Christ through the traditional motif of prophet, priest, and king.

The Call to Ministry: Its Meaning and Scope

George Peck

What I have to offer in this essay is an experiment in thought, having to do with the meaning of ministry in and for the church. I am convinced we are at a point in the Christian community at which we must drastically reconsider our theology of the ministry. My purpose here is to offer a programmatic sketch of some elements that I believe must figure in such a reconsideration. I shall begin with a glimpse of where I propose to go, and then I shall develop the details in more expansive fashion.

My real theme (my not-very-hidden agenda) is "the Christian *laity's* calling to ministry." But I do not think we shall get far with this subject until we deal with the calling to ministry as such. Our common habit in the church is to launch a discussion of ministry with a consideration of the ministry of the ordained—as if that type were the purest, proper form of the ministry—and only thereafter to discuss other kinds of ministry such as the ministry of the laity. My intention is to suggest another approach. I believe we shall make better progress if we first examine the concept of ministry as it applies to the whole people and then look at different types of ministry as specific cases of this application, including the ministry of the ordained. Only in this way, it seems to me, can we avoid inevitably speaking of the ministry of the laity as something secondary and inferior to the ministry of the ordained.

Then, by way of preparation, I want to stress one other issue. In this essay I really do intend to speak of our calling to ministry. There was a time when I thought we could simply say that the word "ministry" meant "service" (*diakonia*), and since all Christians were obviously called to service, all were called to ministry. But I am becoming more and more dissatisfied with that approach. In our usage, "ministry" is not only a general word of this kind; it also has a specific connotation. It refers to something to which people are called in a particular way. That call has to be recognized after testing, and those who are judged to have been called are set apart by the church for a special task or series of tasks. So while all serve in some way, not all are necessarily in fact "ministers." It is that distinction which I want to get into focus. I want to try to make the case that such a call to ministry must be expected for every Christian, not just for those who would be expected to go through the process that leads to what we now refer to as ordination.

I shall present my case by, first, setting out in summary form some biblical and historical considerations in an effort to lay foundations for my argument. Then, on this basis, I shall offer some observations toward an understanding of the meaning of ministry.

Some Biblical and Historical Considerations

We begin with the Old Testament. Here the fundamental datum is the election of Israel, the calling of the whole community to the acknowledgment, worship, and service of God. All the people were called to this. To be an Israelite meant to be subject to the call. But within that general call, some were summoned further by God to specific roles: leaders (Moses), soldiers (Joshua), judges (Gideon, Deborah), priests (Aaron), kings (David), prophets (Elijah, Isaiah). *All* had a call as part of the people; *all* were called to serve the Lord in their positions among the people. *Some* were *specially* called to be accountable in a particular way as those whom God had chosen to play significant roles.

Now let us move to the New Testament. Here again the concept of "call" (*klēsis*) is prominent. Obviously every Christian, every member of the church, has a call into the body of Christ, into relationship with God in Christ. Every believer is summoned to repentance, to faith, to sanctification, to Christian living. It is assumed, and sometimes explicitly stated, that this calling will be worked out in the ordinary affairs of life: in whatever station a person was placed (slave, free, master, servant, husband, wife, merchant) he or she was to live so as to honor the calling in Christ (e.g. Colossians 3:22-24; Ephesians 6:5-9). Whatever one did was done to the glory of God. Then within the community, within the church, special gifts were given to the members. These gifts were related to tasks that needed to be performed: prophets, evangelists, healers, administrators, teachers, and so on (e.g. 1 Corinthians 12:22-30; Ephesians 4:1-6; 1 Peter 4:10-11).

In other words, there is the same overall pattern as in the Old Testament: the call to membership, the call to serve, then specific calls to particular responsibilities for which the members are accountable. However, one notable difference between the Old Testament and the New Testament seems to be that in the latter, in principle, *every* believer has a specific call to a particular task, since every Christian has received a "gift" from the Spirit.

In sketching the biblical material in so summary a manner, I do not want to leave the impression that the move from Scripture to our situation is a simple one. For one thing, I am presenting these ideas in broad sweeps, and many nuances are being ignored. Also, most significantly, the circumstances in which the Bible arose are substantially different from those with which we have to deal. The result is that we cannot hope to find in Scripture a ready-made manual of theology and practice to be followed point by point. The Old Testament speaks of Israel as a people and a nation and can hardly be taken as an item-by-item guide for what we are after. Similarly, the New Testament documents were written in an environment in which the world was not expected to continue for very long and, therefore, do not develop a complete and final vision of the ministry of the people of God in the kind of complex situations that emerged with the passing of time (e.g., 1 Corinthians 7:29-31). All of this must be kept in mind as we try to apply biblical images and concepts to our circumstances. It is inevitable that we shall have to move beyond them, even as we also try to ground our thought in them.

In making this "move beyond," I believe we can be instructed in worthwhile ways by observing what happened to some of the ideas that concern us as the church went through historical changes. After the New Testament period when the expectation of Christ's immediate return had faded and the church grew and spread, a peculiar development took place. As we have noted, it was originally assumed that one's calling to be a Christian would be fulfilled in the midst of life. A person stayed in one's station and lived worthily, as he or she had been summoned to do in Christ. But as the standards of entry into the church dropped with the expansion of Christianity, this expectation of fulfilling a call became virtually meaningless.

When being a Christian became synonymous with being a citizen, many in the church became convinced that really to be Christian, really to fulfill one's calling in Christ, one had to withdraw from the world at large and seek a controlled environment in monastic communities. Eventually, with the multiplication and diversification of special orders in the church in the Middle Ages, it became a common belief that the only people in the strict sense who had a "calling" (vocation) were the monastics, the members of mendicant orders, and the clergy (i.e., monks, nuns, friars, parish priests, and the ecclesiastical hierarchy). The ordinary people did not have time and were too involved in compromising circumstances to fulfill a Christian "calling" in the proper sense. So, above them were ranged those with "vocation" who could pray, worship, discipline themselves, and, in general, respond to Christ's call as it was set forth in Scripture. The result was a striking transformation of the convictions with which the church had begun.

But with the Reformation came an equally notable about-face. Martin Luther demanded a return to the biblical understanding of "call," and "vocation" was again applied to all believers: everyone is "called" to Christ. But in insisting on this, Luther also gave the concept a special twist (for which there was already in Scripture at least a basic precedent): The vocation, the calling of all in Christ, must be worked out in that particular sphere in which each is placed. Thus, the clericalizing of the idea of vocation was radically contradicted. *Every* Christian had a vocation, not only those who were called to churchly tasks (such as preachers and bishops); even purely worldly, secular occupations were to be, and should be, treated as Christian vocations. Christians were to "work out their salvation" not by fleeing to monasteries or into orders, but by doing properly and well, for the sake of Christ, the job they were given in society to do. For Luther, the only persons who *didn't* have a vocation were the monks and nuns who were cut off from the world!

John Calvin later developed a view of vocation that was similar in many respects to Luther's. But with Calvin came also one very important difference. For Luther, society had been ordered by God into a fixed hierarchy of callings, and the responsibility of the Christian was to stay where one was put, where one began, and there to do one's best. Each person had a station in life, determined by birth and family situation, and the Christian vocation was to realize that station as completely as possible.

Calvin was not of this opinion. In his judgment, God deals with people in such a way that they can expect, if they have the ability, to move from one calling to another, especially to move to a "better" calling as a sign of God's blessing. Agreeing with Luther, Calvin thought that the Christian fulfills his or her Christian life and profession in a specific task, even if it is a secular task. But in Calvin's view Christians should not so much accept submissively what had been ordered beforehand as strive through the exercise of their "callings" to improve and develop the society of which they are a part. The task of the Christian in the world is to seek to build the Holy Commonwealth, to build society in accordance with the image of the kingdom. (In New England with the Puritans we have as good an example as can be cited of the way in which some Calvinists tried to work out this understanding of vocation in relation to society.)

Now it is obvious that Luther and Calvin profoundly affected our contemporary secular concepts as well as those of the church. We still speak in common parlance of a person's "vocation" or "calling," and we mean his or her daily work. And there is no doubt that these Reformation views led to a much broader notion of the calling to the Christian community than was in place during the Middle Ages. But it should be noted that they do not in themselves provide a completely satisfactory conception of ministry for the church today.

There is a general call that is to be lived out in particular occupations in society. But ministry still tends to be thought of strictly in terms of what goes on *in the church*. There are orders and levels of ministry within the fellowship of believers (preachers, teachers, deacons, elders, and so on), but ministry more or less stops there. And that point is, by and large, where most of our Protestant denominations have been left and find themselves now.

My proposal in this essay is that it is time for us to try to move a step beyond this limited understanding.

Observations Toward an Understanding of Ministry

To begin with, let me make as clear as I can what I mean by "ministry." I am acknowledging the *general* call to all to fulfill their discipleship in particular vocations, professions, or jobs. All are called to serve Christ where they are: mechanics, lawyers, homemakers, secretaries, politicians, doctors, coal miners, and so on. This insight of the Reformers is to be treasured and continually reaffirmed. It is rooted in the exhortations of the New Testament: "Whatever you are doing, whether you speak or act, do everything in the name of the Lord Jesus . . ." (Colossians 3:17, NEB).

But beyond that general call is ministry. The call to ministry is a *specific* thing that comes in the midst of the general call to discipleship and is linked to a number of distinct elements. It is issued to all believers, in different ways, and for different purposes. In reality it is heard only by some, and among those who hear it, only some are ready to respond and are prepared for what is involved. What then is involved? In spelling this out, the concept of ministry I have in mind will come into focus.

Once a person is called into Christ, (only Christians are called to ministry), the following factors must be identified:

—a personal sense of the Spirit's call to a particular sphere of service;

—the presence of particular gifts;

—the presence of particular occasions for their use;

—preparation for the use of these gifts (usually including education);

—recognition of the particular call by others who are competent, especially the recognition by the church;
—commissioning and appointing by the church;
—support and accountability: being undergirded in and held to account for the exercise of ministry.

It is essential to my point that ministry so conceived can be exercised both *within* the church and *outside* the church (i.e., within the work and worship of the gathered community of believers and within the secular order of life and society). Let me illustrate the idea of ministry in both spheres.

Within the church, there are many areas of ministry for which men and women can be called, prepared, recognized, appointed, supported, and held accountable. These include preaching, celebrating the sacraments, teaching, custodial roles with respect to the gospel and the tradition, service tasks, and ministries of caring. It will be clear at once that this is where those we now ordain usually fulfill their ministry. But it is basic to my understanding of ministry that these ministries should not necessarily be limited to such persons. Theologically, in principle, these ministries are available to all believers, and the church would be the richer if they were "shared" more widely.

But that having been said, it is important to call to mind what is involved in their being regarded as "ministries." I am not referring just to getting people to volunteer or simply to "substitute for the pastor." I am talking about recognized types of ministry within the congregation for which there are structures related to the factors listed earlier. If people are to minister, as I am conceiving of ministry, there must be calling, gifts, preparation, recognition, commissioning, support, and accountability on the part of the one called *and* of the church. Such a level of seriousness is at present hardly discernible in any denomination.

But it is of particular importance to our subject that we speak also of ministry in the so-called "secular" sphere. Here is where we move into territory little trodden by the historic church. We have long acknowledged that there can be vocation in secular professions and jobs. These are areas in which our Christian calling can be fulfilled in service. But are they spheres of "ministry" as I am envisaging ministry? I want to contend that they can and should be, though again it will mean our taking "ministry" with a special seriousness.

My case can probably be seen most easily if we take an instance from one of the "caring" professions. Here is a young person who wants to be a doctor. She has the talents needed, a strong sense of call to such ministry, and goes to school with that call in mind. She graduates and enters the medical profession. Now why should she not be specifically recognized and appointed or commissioned by the church for ministry as a doctor? Why should there not be special structures of support and accountability for such a person? And if it should seem strange that I press the matter, I simply draw attention to the fact that we have done precisely this very thing for generations with all kinds of people who have gone to serve as overseas missionaries! Doctors, nurses, agriculturalists, teachers, nutritionists, builders, social workers. . . . We see nothing at all peculiar about asking such persons to submit to our structures of ministry when we send them abroad in the employ of a church body, but for some reason we draw back when the homeland is the sphere of their labors and they earn their bread from someone else's budget. But there is no inherent ground for such discrimination.

I realize that the point is always more easily seen when professions like those I have cited are in question. And I am conscious that a good deal of work has yet to be done to make clear what it means for bus drivers, assembly-line workers, and garbage collectors to be included. I am also very conscious that I do not here have space to investigate just what the *content* of ministry in my sense is. What makes a bus driver or a nutritionist who is a *minister* (called, prepared, recognized, commissioned, held accountable) different from a bus driver or a nutritionist who is not? Does he or she act differently, say special kinds of things, take particular sorts of stands, adopt definable attitudes, life-styles? I believe the answer is affirmative in each case, and one of the most important tasks yet before us is to explore what all an affirmative answer means. For the moment, I must assume that identifying lay ministries can be done. Meanwhile, I want to press for a response to the concept of ministry that I am enunciating. The nub of my argument is this: If a person is willing to undertake the discipline and the commitment, why should not the church affirm and structure itself for this kind of ministry just as much as it does now with respect to what we call the ministry of the ordained?

Conclusion

In conclusion, in order to make what I am saying somewhat sharper, let me draw out very briefly two specific implications.

First, within the church, I am calling for a particular role for those who are now "ordained" ministers, but I am seeking also to extend the concept of ministry significantly beyond them. In my view the task of the ordained is to see to it that the various ministries of the community are properly carried out, both inside and outside the church. This will involve such tasks as challenging, teaching, initiating, and it will be crucial to the life of the church that the work be done well. In a sense, as leaders and pastors, such persons will be primarily responsible for knowing the gospel and the tradition and for calling the fellowship to worship, study, and action, even though these persons will always be "first among equals" but not first in any absolute way. (Perhaps the closest analogy to what I have in mind is the role, according to Calvin, of "teaching elders.")

But it is crucial that such persons not assume that the ministries of the church ought to be carried out by them alone. On the contrary, within the church there ought to be a variety of ministries fulfilled by a variety of people, ministry being understood as I have defined it. I am urging that we look to the training, acknowledging, and commissioning of *many* people in our congregations for the several tasks that now must be carried out, including leading worship, teaching, preaching, celebrating the sacraments, caring.

In other words, I am arguing that there should be a greatly expanded understanding of the ministry of the laity that goes beyond the notion of recruiting people to "help the minister" on a volunteer basis. What I have in mind is something like an "order" of ministers within the community, to which the present "ordained" ministers would belong, but which would not be limited exclusively to them. Indeed, if we were to move in this direction, we probably would find ourselves at a certain point having to rethink the concept of ordination altogether. But that issue I must leave for another time.

Second, I am pressing for very special attention to *ministry in the "secular" world*. Again I believe we must consider the establishment of a special "order" for people called, recognized, and commissioned for such roles. These would be "ministries of *outreach*" as distinct from the ministries directed to the internal life of the Christian body. It is here, perhaps above all, that we are moving (in fact, though not in principle) beyond the New Testament which, given its eschatological orientation, did not develop such a notion to any extent. We are also, I believe, moving beyond the position of the Reformers as well. Despite their stress on vocation in the world, they limited the concept of ministry rather strictly to the inner life of the church.

In making the shift for which I am calling, it is important that we keep in mind again the particular way in which I am speaking of "ministry." It is not simply that everyone is a minister, whatever he or she does. Everyone is called to Christ and to serve Christ in daily tasks and professions. But for ministry, in whatever form or mode, there is a *special* call, and there is training, recognition, commissioning, support, and accountability. If we should take this direction, clearly we would need new structures of ministry within the church, and we would have to deal with many questions about content, organization, and the like. We would also have to face the challenge of new possibilities for Christian education and training. But in a world as complex and troubled as ours, it could be that it is precisely to this kind of fresh vision that we are driven by the Spirit.

Let me once more, by way of summary, review the basic concepts that constitute the framework for the position I have been developing:

1. There is a *general* call to *all* to membership in Christ.

2. *All* Christians have a responsibility to live a life of discipleship in their daily tasks and in the fellowship of the church.

3. There is a variety of *ministries* that all should undertake, both within the church and in the secular world. For these ministries the church needs special structures for training, recognition, commissioning, support, and accountability.

4. What we now call the ordained ministry is one type of ministry within this variety, albeit a very important type.

My contention is that only on such a basis as indicated by these factors will we really take seriously the matter of the call of the laity to ministry. And in the process of working through the many issues that demand attention, I believe we shall immeasurably enrich our understanding of ministry as such. Both the gospel and the times seem to me to require the effort.

A Holy Priesthood

M. B. Handspicker

Ministry in and of the church is ordered in many different ways. These differences have often arisen from faithful response to different historical and social circumstances. Variety in ministry began even within New Testament times. The same can be said about church order, and Hans Küng said about doctrine:

> The Scripture itself shows us that the *one* Faith can live in *different* formulas. One and the same good news is reported by four Evangelists in very different ways; one and the same Lord is described in very different terms as regards his glory and his humiliation; the words of institution of the one and the same Eucharist are given in different ways. . . . But the fundamental conviction remained that no one formula could suffice to account for the whole fullness of the Faith, and that difference in *formula* did not necessarily involve a difference in *faith*. [1]

Within the New Testament we have the early "communalism" of Acts, the charismatically ordered Pauline communities, the conciliar motifs of Paul visiting the apostles and elders in Jerusalem, and the more highly structured communities described in the Pastoral Epistles.

Neither the different formulas of faith nor the various ways of ordering church life were matters that *divided* the early church. Küng then raised the question "How do we get from the New Testament Canon, which remains one despite its lack of unity, to confessional multiplicity?" He answered ruefully, "By *choice*."

That is, by not seriously accepting the Canon as one thing, for all its lack of unity; by not striving through all the difficulties confronting each other in it, to reach a *comprehensive* understanding of it. By using the lack of unity in the Canon to make a selection from the Canon. [2]

By merely choosing *one* formulation of faith or *one* way of ordering church life as normative, we miss coming to grips with Scripture as a whole. In short, we are "heretics." Yet, faced with such multiplicity, what are we to do?

One way of answering would be to say that faced with such a range of choices, the church is permitted to have as diverse a range of doctrinal formulas and approaches to ordering the church as there are in Scripture. Negatively formulated, this would mean that one should not, in the church, enforce any narrow range of order in the name of truth or orthodoxy. In short, Scripture *permits* a variety of ordering within the one church and does not *prescribe* any one as normative. Is it then merely a matter of "you pay your money and you make your choice?" Let us first note some historical developments since New Testament times and then return to this question.

Historical Development

There is not enough space here to trace the various developments of church order; we shall for the most part merely note some of them. With Ignatius we see the development of a monarchial episcopate; here was tight control of a community under persecution, a community that chose to witness rather than to go underground. After the church's acceptance in the Roman Empire, at the prodding of the Emperor Constantine, ecumenical councils (meetings of bishops from all over the empire) met to settle disputed matters of faith and draw up canons to govern church life. By the time of the late Middle Ages a grand hierarchical vision of the universe, of church and society, had fully developed.

With the coming of the Reformation many different orderings of church life developed: the republican theocracy of Calvin and his heirs in the Reformed wing of the church, Luther's emphasis on "sound doctrine" and a rather more indifferent attitude towards order, the convinced congregationalists' conventicles of the Radical Reformation on the Continent, and the Brownists in England. In Europe "*Landeskirch-*

en" ("Landed church," i.e., the parish or community of a church) developed, each region having its own tradition — Reformed, Lutheran, Roman Catholic — and even today remnants of that organizational approach exist. In the United States the "denomination" developed as still another form of church life in a pluralistic society. Finally, in recent times, the conciliar movement on local, national, and international levels has developed cooperative forms of church life.

Present Questions

Today we find that as heirs of these developments we have a wide variety of ways of ordering church life before us. They are often competitive and mutually exclusive, although the ecumenical movement since 1910 has brought us greater understanding of one another's structures. In our historical circumstances the question faces us that also faced our forebears: how can we faithfully order church life today? Is it merely a matter of choosing? No. Our contention is that New Testament and historical studies reveal there are principles that should guide our choice, although they need not dictate that there is "one and only one" way of ordering church life.

First, we need Right Order. The church needs to be so ordered that sound doctrine and practice are preserved. Second, we need Good Order. Order needs to serve the mission and purpose of the church: the Good News needs to be spread in word and deed. Finally, we need Fit Order. The ordering of the church's life needs to be appropriate to its life in a particular time and place.

Using these principles as our guides, we shall argue for two major points of ordering church life today in the United States. First, conducting the sacramental ministry of the church, especially presiding at the celebration of Communion, is in principle open to any member of the church by virtue of his or her baptism. Second, a major reassessment of the role of the professionally trained minister is necessary, and that role's primary function should be the promotion of sound teaching and the exercise of discipline within the community.

An Unusual Religion

We shall begin our exploration by looking at the character of the Christian community as it is presented to us in the New

Testament. One scholar refers to the church as "a-cultic," indicating that little attention was paid to elaborating the ritual of the community, unlike other religions of the time. Yet the church was a community "directed to the worship of God." In the dialectic between these two characteristics we may find clues concerning the nature of the church that can guide our reflection about the meaning of order and ordination for the church today.

An interesting place to begin our examination is with the Letter to the Hebrews. This is both the most "priestly" and the most "a-cultic" writing in the New Testament. Christ is celebrated as our high priest throughout this writing. In many ways the climactic affirmation of the book is the statement: "He has appeared once for all at the end of the age to put away sin by the sacrifice of himself" (Hebrews 9:26b). Christ is the high priest to end all priesthood; his sacrifice once for all has done away with the need for sacrifice to be offered again.

Yet this does not do away with the need for worship. The author writes: ". . . Let us offer to God acceptable worship, with reverence and awe; for our God is a consuming fire" (Hebrews 12:28-29). In the very next verse a clue to this "acceptable worship" is given: "Let brotherly love continue" (Hebrews 13:1). In the whole sweep of the book's argument, in the mounting of example after example of faith—faith acted out often in heroic deed—it is clear that the "acceptable worship" of God is to "lay aside every weight, and sin which clings so closely, and . . . run with perseverance the race that is set before us" (Hebrews 12:1). The way believers live their lives, individually and corporately, is the way they worship God.

For the author of Hebrews, the fundamental act of *cultic* worship has been accomplished by Christ with his sacrifice. ("Cultic" and "cult" are used here as they originally are defined: a system of religious beliefs and ritual or adherents to this system.) All subsequent worship is lived out by believers in the "brotherly love" of community and in running "the race that is set before us," in living Christian lives in the world.

While little in this epistle speaks about church order, it is clear that the author did not think of an anarchic community. He exhorts his hearers: "Obey your leaders and submit to them; for they are keeping watch over your souls, as [persons] who will have to give account" (Hebrews 13:17). (Their "accountability" may, by the way, give us at least one principle by which to evaluate leadership in the church.) These leaders, *hegoumenoi*, may have been the prophets or apostles who preached the gospel to the readers of the epistle. It is interesting to note that the term *hegoumenoi* is not a cultic one; it seems to refer to the task of discipline rather than to a leadership function in worship. Whatever "worship" is, it is the function of the entire community.

But is this approach merely idiosyncratic with the author of Hebrews? In many ways Hebrews seems to be an odd book in the New Testament; is it also odd in its attitude toward cult and community leadership?

First Peter

A similar attitude toward the need for total community involvement is shared by the author of First Peter when he declares: "But you are a chosen race, a royal priesthood, a holy nation, God's own people, that you may declare the wonderful deeds of him who called you out of darkness into his marvelous light" (1 Peter 2:9). While there *are* leaders in the New Testament communities, nowhere are they called "priests." This term refers only to Christ (in Hebrews) or to the whole people of God (in 1 Peter, Revelation 1:6, 5:10, 20:6).[3] In the case of Christ his priesthood consists not only in offering the sacrifice but in his *being* the sacrifice.

For Christians also, the sacrifice they offer is themselves. They are a royal priesthood offering "spiritual sacrifices." In First Peter the character of these sacrifices is outlined in 2:11-16: "abstain from the passions of the flesh"; "maintain good conduct among the Gentiles"; "be subject . . . to every human institution"; "live as free men, yet without using your freedom as a pretext for evil; but live as servants of God."

Clearly for the author of First Peter, as for the author of Hebrews, Christian "worship," the "sacrifice" offered to God, is a life lived out faithfully in the "world." Christians run the "race," not primarily in the community, but in their worldly occupations and living.

Paul

Paul also makes the personal and incarnational character of sacrifice compellingly clear in a verse we often read but do not take literally enough: "I appeal to you therefore, brethren, by the mercies of God, to present your *bodies* as a living sacrifice, holy and acceptable to God, which is your spiritual worship" (Romans 12:1, author's emphasis). Ephesians also seems to parallel the offering of Christ and our own offerings: "And walk in love, as Christ loved us and gave himself for us, a fragrant offering and sacrifice to God" (Ephesians 5:2).

Christians are to put their bodies (*somata*), their full selves, on the line as a sacrifice. The corporate character of these united individual efforts is indicated by the shift from plural to singular. This effort is the worship of the community, the investment of the faithful in "the Way." The priesthood of all is the living out of life as Christians and is not limited to the inner churchly life of the community.

Yet there is an *order* to the life within this priestly community. In Romans 12 Paul indicates that each person is given a gift (*charis*); he or she is to use it "according to the measure of faith" (*kata ten analogian tes pisteos*) given him or her. Acting in this manner, all of our "bodies" become harmoniously operative as "members" of the "body of Christ." There is no pure egalitarianism here; gifts differ and functions differ. The lists differ in content and in order (Romans 12:3-8; 1 Corinthians 12:8-31). Paul speaks of "first apostles, second prophets, third teachers" and then lists numerous other gifts. What priority there is resides in those gifts that have the particular function of ministering the Word. This would also fit in with Paul's criterion that the gifts are to be used to edify the church (1 Corinthians 12:7; 14:1-5) and testify to Jesus as the Lord (12:3).

Of all the gifts of which Paul speaks, however, none refers to liturgical leadership. (The closest, service—*diakonia*—in Romans 12:7, seems better to be read in its more specific sense of the administration of alms and bodily service. [4]) In reading through First Corinthians and noting the difficulty Paul had in dealing with the derelictions in that community connected with the Lord's Supper, one is struck by the fact that

Paul has no one person or group of persons to hold responsible for eucharistic discipline—except the whole community.
This is the more surprising since Paul's discussion of the
"gifts" comes immediately after his exhortations concerning
behavior at the Supper. One would expect that if one of the
charismata were liturgical leadership or presidency, Paul would
mention it here.

When we turn to the rest of the New Testament, we find the
same state of affairs. *Nowhere* are special ministers of the
sacraments mentioned. Even in the Pastoral Epistles, with
their emphasis on order in the face of challenge (from Gnosticism?), Timothy and Titus are urged to preach right doctrine
and, even more, to live—and make sure other leaders (bishops, deacons, elders, widows) live—exemplary lives. We would
have to make a very large assumption, with no positive evidence, were we to assume that those leaders (*hegoumenoi*)—
apostles, prophets, or others—were presidents at liturgical
services as well as being entrusted with preaching the Word
and embodying the Word in life. Rather, the indications are
that the people as a whole, the congregation in each place,
is celebrant of the Supper. There may have been some kind
of presidency, but it seems not to have been an office or even
a particular gift.

Yet from an investigation of the worship life of the early
Christian church, we discover that their services were rich in
the elements that were included. The basic service consisted
of sermon, prayer, and supper. From the Pauline corpus we
also hear of psalms and hymns, revelation, speaking in
tongues, and interpretation of tongues. The inclusion of ben-
edictions and doxologies as well as early confessional sum-
maries in Paul's letters leads us to suspect that these two were
elements of early Christian worship. [5] Nowhere do we find any
indication of a set order, except that it appears that the supper
came after the preaching. [6] The various elements—set liturgical prayers or confessions, reading from Scripture, sermon,
and relatively free expressions of the Spirit—need not all occur
every time. In the Pauline communities their occurrence would
depend upon the distribution of gifts in a given locality.

In worship, as in community life generally, the ordering
principle for Paul is threefold: that all be done to testify to

Jesus as Lord; that all things edify, build up the community as the body of Christ; and that all be done in love. If there be any priority in Paul's thought, it is the preaching of the Word. "How are they to hear without a preacher?" he questions in Romans 10:14, and he speaks of the (temporal?) priority of apostles, prophets, and teachers in 1 Corinthians 12:28. When, in the Pastoral Epistles, the community seeks greater control in the face of the challenge of Gnosticism, the priority again is on the establishment of officers who will function to keep doctrine and life pure. Here there is no mention of their functioning in particular ways in the liturgical life of the community—except that the fundamental "liturgy" of the community was to be its faithful following of "the Way."

Principles of Church Order

From this survey of New Testament materials we need to discover if there is support for the principles we articulated earlier. Even Paul, for all the charismatic character of the communities that he addressed, insisted that all things be done "decently and in order." The church is not an anarchy; it is a community, and while *various* ways of ordering its life may be permitted, its life *must* be ordered, organized. Insofar as any priority exists in Paul's lists of gifts or in the offices mentioned in the Pastoral Epistles, that priority is based on keeping *doctrine* and *life* pure. In terms of our principles, this means that there must be Right Order.

Also the church must be organized in such a way that its priestly character is capable of being lived out, its mission of service undergirded, and its prophetic words proclaimed. This mission of the church means that there must be Good Order. These two principles finally need to be given more specific content in terms of the situation in which a church finds itself historically. When this task is faithfully accomplished, we shall have Fit Order.

In addition to these formal principles are three material principles that we can gather from our earliest review of the New Testament literature. (1) All gifts are essential to the community and should be able to be utilized, supported, and valued. There *is* functional subordination, but this means that leadership may well shift from time to time, depending upon what the community needs or what tasks it is undertaking. Authority, in short, needs to be achieved (through recognition of gifts) rather than merely ascribed (due to office alone). (2) The community needs to be ordered so that its central activity, worship, can be performed regularly and in such a fashion that the priestly character of the *whole* community is manifest. (3) The "traditioning" of the faith must occur. All must come to know the lore of the community; some may take this task of learning and passing on of the tradition as a particular vocation within the community.

A Model for Today

Many kinds of ordering of the church's community life have existed in every age. These range from a local congregation's committees, task forces, and study groups, upward to associations, synods, conferences, boards, and instrumentalities. Today the multiplicity extends to ecumenical organization, *ad hoc* social action task forces, and coalitions formed around various issues, as Christians order themselves to fulfill their calling in this day and age.

What I wish to propose now as a model for ordering our life today arises out of the study I have made of the New Testament and from several convictions about what our churches need today to be more effective as enablers of the whole people of God.

The convictions are these. First, while we are a "kingdom of priests," we have lost the sense of what this means and we need to recover it. The church is "the sacrament of Christ"; as Christ's body we are called to incarnate God's love and grace and judgment in the world. As such we need to be fed sacramentally, and, therefore, Word and sacrament are central to our corporate life. We should be able to come to worship expecting to hear the Word proclaimed in Scripture, song, and sermon; we should be able to come to worship expecting to be nourished by the "visible Word" of Christ's presence in the sacrament; we should be able to come to worship and experience *ourselves* as priests in a kingdom of priests.

Second, while we have a tradition of "learned ministry" and ordain and install our clergy as pastors and teachers, the clergy today are undergoing an identity crisis. While they are called upon to be everything from baby-sitters to administrators, pastoral counselors to janitors, hand holders to prophets, there seems to be no central focus to their task. With the emerging movement of the ministry of the laity, this identity crisis seems to be exacerbated even further; clergy ask themselves, "If everyone is a 'minister,' what does it mean that *I* am an 'ordained' minister?" The last vestige of distinction seems to be that only clergy are allowed to celebrate the sacrament in most of our churches. Yet this does not take four years of college and three years of seminary to learn to do. What I am going to propose may seem to take even this last vestige of identity away, but I believe that what we can accomplish is a much needed reidentification of both laity and clergy in their proper roles in the "kingdom of priests."

Priests and Bishops

Since in the New Testament evidence we are called priests, I can see no compelling reason why the celebration of sacraments has to be reserved to a professional group within the church. Baptism *is* ordination; by virtue of it we are made members of a holy priesthood. It confers an indelible character upon us; we are "priest for ever, after the order of Melchizedek." When we are gathered around the table, we need someone to preside over our meal; but we all together have what Roman Catholics term a "liturgical apostolate." The *community* is the priesthood (which may well be why the New Testament writers made no mention of who "presided" at the eucharist). This further implies that since all are priests, *in principle* any member of the church can preside at our meals; and in order to manifest this principle, the hosts at the eucharist ought to vary from celebration to celebration.

Such a practice could help make clear to each of us that our *lives* are ministries; we are called to present our bodies as a living sacrifice. There is no special priesthood apart from the priesthood of all. Such an ordering of our lives would incarnate in church order the Reformation affirmation of the "priesthood of all believers" and be true to the New Testament evidence we have examined earlier. Such a move would include laity in the "ministry of identity" of which Gabriel Fackre speaks. [7] (Fackre identifies clergy as ministers of identity, laity as ministers of vitality.)

More importantly, however, each of us "priestly people" would then be called more clearly to view our daily work as ministry as well, with all the possibilities and problems that such a viewing might entail. Can I consider myself a priest of the church of Christ engaged in the work I do? It might be, and I believe it is, easier for garbage collectors to say yes to this question than some people in the advertising world. If I *am* one of the "ministers of identity" in the Christian community, my "ministry of vitality"[8] may be clearer to me than were I, as most of us presently are, excluded from that role.

What, then, is the role of "professional clergy"? Ought we to have such an office in the church? I believe that the answer to the second question is "Yes!" and that the New Testament can give us clues to the character of such an office. The New Testament communities had definite leaders whose function was definite also. They had the special responsibilities in the community of preserving the faith, maintaining continuity, and interpreting the faith in changing circumstances. We have seen this character of leadership in the Pauline lists of gifts, in the role of *hegoumenoi* (leaders) in the Letter to the Hebrews, and in the description of the role of bishops in the Pastoral Epistles. In this regard it may be that our practice in preparing women and men for the ordained ministry is better than our present theory about ordination. We have required a learned ministry: persons must receive college and seminary training. Seminaries are not vocational schools; the bulk of the time in any curriculum is, happily, spent in learning the "lore" through work in Scripture, history, theology, and ethics. And this needs to become, much more than it is at present, the focus of clerical identity.

While it is not the sole responsibility of clergy to maintain the tradition, they are set apart, as were Talmudic scholars in Jewish communities, to ensure that the tradition is kept. (In those communities that have no set-apart and learned ministry, what becomes the responsibility of all often becomes the responsibility of too few or of none at all.) A United Church of Christ document on "sound teaching" puts the case well:

Pastors, in concert with laity under the guidance of the Holy Spirit, function as (a) stewards of tradition, (b) shapers of sound teaching, (c) clarifiers and interpreters of the present human condition, and (d) personal examples of faithfulness in daily life.[9]

The last phrase in this statement indicates another dimension of the pastoral function: pastors are to *live out* the tradition. This means merely that clergy *must* be what *all* are called to be. First and foremost, of course, this means to live as forgiven sinners who continually need to receive God's grace because of their weakness. It means to exemplify and confess the human struggle, not to try to live above it. Second, it means to live lives devoted to perseverance in building Christian character, informed by the ethics of the Christian community. (A sign that clergy and seminary students are perceiving this role as authentic is the increasing interest in what is called "spiritual formation.")

Finally, clergy are called in their role as maintainers of the tradition to exercise oversight (*episcope*) in the life of the church. While all are in principle permitted to preside at the Eucharist or celebrate baptism, the community expects its clergy to oversee and supervise this process since the sacraments *are* the "visible Word." It is a matter of training people from within the community for this function. Again the teaching role of the clergy becomes clear. As a *servum servorum Dei* ("servant of the servants of God") he or she enables the priesthood to function effectively.

Summary

In brief we can list the highlights of our study.

1. Fundamentally, Christian life is corporate. Paul speaks of offering our *bodies* as a living sacrifice. The whole people is priestly. This priesthood is given the body because it *is* the body of Christ and Christ is the one High Priest. The essential worship of this priestly people is living life in the everyday world, reinforced by the worship (*leitourgia*) of the community.

2. All gifts (*charismata*) to the Christian community are essential to its life. Each person is to use the gift according to the measure of faith given him or her, and none is to think more highly of himself or herself that he or she ought to think.

Humility, love, edification of the community, and testimony to the Lord are the ordering principles of community life.

3. Worship within the community is a multifaceted activity, a mixture of set forms and spiritual freedom. It can vary from place to place according to the gifts of each community.

4. Overseeing, or *episcope*, is a necessary function within the life of the community. We can best summarize our study by quoting again from the document on sound teaching:

> [There is] a continuing need for the function within our polity of (a) responsible "episcopacy" entrusted to oversee not only finances, programs, and the organizations, but also sound teaching of the church, and (b) a responsible teaching office of designated persons who, by sustained grappling with major theological issues, call the church to be faithful to its biblical heritage in performing its mission. [10]

In line with New Testament and Reformation teaching we have proposed to eliminate not the clergy but the laity. In the church there are no lay people. In our baptism we have all been ordained "priest for ever, after the order of Melchizedek." But we have not abolished differentiation within the clergy. What we have proposed may be compared with the model of the early church under the superintendance of the bishop. Our "bishops" have the task of overseeing the work of the "kingdom of priests" and serving the holy priesthood as "theologians in residence," working and teaching *in* and *for* the *laos* of God. When this is understood, other tasks of the professional clergy can be seen in proper perspective. Administration, counseling, preaching are all ways they further their fundamental task of teaching the faith and its implications for personal and corporate life in today's changing world.

Notes

[1] Hans Küng, *The Living Church*, trans. Cecily Hastings and N.D. Smith (London: Sheed and Ward, 1963), p. 306.

[2] *Ibid.*, pp. 260-261.

[3] The only possible exception to this is Paul's remark in Romans 15:16 in which he refers to his mission "to be a minister of Christ Jesus to the Gentiles in the priestly service of the gospel of God, so that the offering of the Gentiles may be acceptable, sanctified by the Holy Spirit." But the "offering" of the Gentiles is "obedience" (verse 18), and this is quite in character with what we have been saying about Hebrews.

[4] W. Sanday and A.C. Headlam, *The Epistle to the Romans*, International

Critical Commentary (New York: Charles Scribner's Sons, 1905), p. 357.

[5] Oscar Cullman, *Early Christian Worship* (Philadelphia: The Westminster Press, 1978), pp. 20 et passim.

[6] Cullman also speculates that the speaking in tongues probably occurred usually in connection with the prayer *Maranatha,* offered up as the climax of the supper. See *ibid.,* p. 21.

[7] See Gabriel Fackre's essay "Christ's Ministry and Ours" immediately following this essay.

[8] *Ibid.*

[9] Office of Church Life and Leadership, United Church of Christ, "Toward the Task of Sound Teaching in the United Church of Christ" (July 1978), p. 5.

[10] *Ibid.*

Christ's Ministry and Ours

Gabriel Fackre

For the past few years a group of people in the Boston science community has been meeting in members' homes. Each evening a different member takes the "hot seat" to talk about his or her work. Frank reported on the breakthroughs in gene splicing in his experiments at MIT. Al tested out with the group a code of ethics he developed for cancer research. Jill described a new strain of corn being studied in her laboratory and the impact it could have on hunger in Third World countries. George told of his misgivings about his company's new MX missile contract. Bill brought charts and graphs to get feedback on his effort to widen employee decision-making power in the small firm he had founded. Sandra explained the dilemmas of many science teachers these days as they struggle with the creationist-evolutionist controversy. Carl shared his attempt to alert fellow pediatricians to the medical effects of a nuclear attack and the need for a freeze on this weaponry. It is in this learning laboratory of real people, members of Eliot Church, Newton, that the proposals which follow have been developed and refined. [1]

What is going on when Frank expresses doubt about the commercialization of gene research or Al urges protection standards for laboratory workers or Jill puts up with the hassles of her job in the interest of its far-reaching benefits?

Are they acts of moral conscience? Indeed. Is it the practicing of one's Christianity? Yes. But something more is happening. It has to do with the answer to the question "Who carries forward the work of Christ?"

In Christian theology the "work of Christ" refers to the service Christ performed for the salvation of the world in his life, death, and resurrection. "The Son of Man also came not to be served but to serve" (Mark 10:45). His work is his *ministry.* As such, Christ is *the* minister. Therefore all those who are called to ministry are the present representatives of who he was and what he did. Christ continues his ministry in their ministry.

Christian tradition has portrayed the work of Jesus Christ as prophet, priest, and king. As prophet he foretells the truth; as priest he makes a sacrifice for our sin; and as king he triumphs over evil and death.

The church has made use of this threefold office of Christ in characterizing the ministry that succeeds Christ's work. In particular, it regularly describes the functions of the clergy in the triple terms. In the Protestant tradition, "pastors are those who are at the head of a definite flock for teaching, administering the sacraments and exercising oversight."[2] In the Roman Catholic tradition, ordination to holy orders confers a threefold power: magisterial, sacerdotal, and jurisdictional.[3] While there are fundamental differences between Protestant and Roman Catholic views on ministry, it is instructive to note the agreement at this point. In both cases the ordained class continue the threefold work of Jesus Christ; what he did in his ministry, they do in their ministry. It is right here that we find the historical and theological roots of inherited notions of clergy and laity.

We shall reexamine in the discussion that follows the Christological foundations for ministry as they are discernible in Scripture and tradition, giving special attention to the themes of the body of Christ and the threefold office, looking for larger meanings than are presently found in received notions of the status and role of Frank and Jill and their friends.

The Body of Christ

We begin with a cluster of New Testament texts that deal with the image of the church as the body of Christ. The people of God together constitute that organism, "many members . . . are one body . . ." (Romans 12:4-5). As befits a body, it "does not consist of one member but of many" (1 Corinthians

12:14). Thus "there is one body and one Spirit . . ." (Ephesians 4:4) that animates this community. Therefore the continuation of Jesus Christ and his ministry in our midst is his body in its *entirety* as it is empowered by his Spirit. In these key passages are materials for reenvisioning the doctrine of ministry.

Identity and Vitality

The Ephesians passage on the body of Christ has been the subject of considerable attention in recent discussions of the ministry of the laity. The debate about "the fatal comma" has eventuated in translations of Ephesians 4:11-12 that render the text, "And his gifts were that some should be apostles, some prophets, some evangelists, some pastors and teachers to equip the saints for the work of ministry . . ." (RSV) or "to equip God's people for work in his service . . ." (NEB). [4] Thus understood, the passage provides reason for (a) extending the concept of ministry to all the members of the body and (b) viewing the particular role of pastors and teachers as that of "equipping the saints."

As valuable as these insights are, this Ephesians text needs to be enriched by themes from Romans 12 and 1 Corinthians 12, for circumstances in these other churches bring into bolder relief other aspects of collegial service. Thus Paul's counsel to the Corinthian congregation, given in the light of inordinate claims made by one or another of the parts of that community, has to do with the two-way traffic of ministry. "The eye cannot say to the hand, 'I have no need of you . . .' " (1 Corinthians 12:21) applies not only to the saints who need equipping from the pastors and teachers, but to the pastors and teachers who need equipping from the saints as well. Empowering moves in two directions. It goes also from helper and healer to prophet and apostle. Earlier views of the relation of clergy to laity do indeed affirm the ministry of the laity but see the relationship as the "ordained ministry" equipping the saints for their work (the clergy as "quartermaster corps" feeding the troops, an earlier often-used figure). This is too simplistic in the light of Pauline description of *mutual* empowerment.

The Corinthian and Roman texts further refine and enrich the apostles-prophets-saints relationship of Ephesians 4 in their accent on the multiplicity of the gifts of the Spirit and, thus, the plurality of nonclerical ministries within the body of Christ. An examination of this range of different services adds significantly to the clarification of the key question we are posing about the relationship of the two subcommunities traditionally referred to as clergy and laity. The services that keep company with apostle, prophet, teacher, and their equivalents—workers of miracles, healers, helpers, administrators, speakers in various tongues, interpreters of tongues, contributors, doers of works of mercy—strongly suggest a pattern of interrelationship. Taken together and interpreted in the setting of the body imagery, the *commonality, particularity,* and *mutuality* of ministry emerge.

Commonality

The commonality of ministry is grounded in the body metaphor itself, that is, the ministry of Christ, which in the source and norm of all Christian ministry is carried forward through the present body of Christ. All of what Christ was on earth then continues to all who compose the body of Christ on earth now. The powers and mandates of ministry are given to the one body by the animating breath of the Spirit. Thus the continuity with Christ comes through the unity of the body of Christ: as one body, all the people of God share in the common gifts and claims. It is in this sense that some of the earlier formulations on the ministry of the laity are to be understood: (a) The people of God are the *laos,* and therefore all members, clergy included, are "the laity." (b) Baptism is the ordination into the ministry of the *laos.* Whatever particularities are acknowledged, therefore, are outgrowths of this common body that lives from the breath of the one Spirit under the work of the one Lord, to which body belongs the primal inheritance of both power and imperative.

Particularity

The particularity is as much a feature of the body image as is the commonality, for bodies are not what they are without the variety of their parts. But the question we have posed about clergy and laity and the character of the multiple gifts point us to a deeper pattern within the pluralism of ministry. Described in the Pauline imagery of these texts are some organs and limbs associated with the *vital signs* of a living self, from beating heart to moving feet. And there are some body parts associated with the *identifying marks* of a particular selfhood, from memory cells to speaking lips. One keeps the body alive and alert, and the other remembers and declares whose body it is.

The signs of life in the earliest Christian community—helping, healing, miracle working, tongues, acts of mercy, serving, contributing—all are ministries of *vitality*. Those reminders within the body of the source of that life—apostle, prophet, pastor, teacher—are the ministries of *identity*.

The gifts of vitality give the body life and locomotion. They empower it to walk and work in the world. They move it in pilgrimage on the way to God's future. As stewards of its *hopes*, they preserve the church from nostalgia. Those members of the body, oriented in their calling to the secular arena (outside the institutional church) whom we have called the "laity," constitute these ministries of vitality. As the *church scattered*, they take the body into the world and are the body in its vital movements of outreach; they are the Spirit's organs of mission.

The gifts of identity give the body self-identification. They empower it to know and to be who it is. As the stewards of its *memories*, they preserve it from amnesia. They point the Christian company to its "whence" so that it may better know its "whither." These members of the body, directed in their calling to the churchly arena and whom we have identified as "the clergy," constitute the ministries of identity. In serving the *church gathered*, they are called to a vocation of empowerment of the community at the place of inreach; they are the Spirit's organs of *nurture*.

Mutuality

The mutuality of ministries is fundamental to their communality and inseparable from their particularity. As parts of a body animated by the breath of the same Spirit, they cannot perform their functions without being in living interrelationship. The head cannot say to the feet, "I have no need of you" (1 Corinthians 12:21). The ministries of identity require the ministries of vitality to carry out the very purposes of identity.

Can Herb preach on Sunday in the most meaningful way to a congregation that includes Carl and Al and Jill if he does not know what happens in their lives on Monday afternoon or, perhaps, has not been helped by them in a Tuesday evening group to ask the right questions of the text he explores in his study on Wednesday morning? And the ministries of vitality require the ministries of identity in order to be the church on their terrain. Can Frank make his most effective witness in his MIT laboratory without the perspective brought by the lore of Scripture and tradition in which Herb is trained and called to share with him in preaching, teaching, and worship?

Mutuality of ministry entails not only the enrichment of each by the other but also the active participation of each in the very being and work of the other. As in the ancient trinitarian doctrine of "perichoresis" in which the Persons in the divine being enjoy their own individuality but at the same time have such a unity that they "coinhere," so the ministries of identity and vitality have a genuine particularity but at the same time live in mutual participation.

George, as longtime advisor of the Eliot Youth Group, has had a very strong influence on a generation of young people. In that outreach role he has performed a ministry of nurture, representing and sharing the identity of Christian faith in the church gathered. Herb, the pastor, on the other hand, is known throughout the city for his active part in community organization of the poor and aged and his leadership in the peace movement. In that outreach role, he performs a ministry of vitality, representing the mission of the church scattered.

There are several ways in which this mutuality and interpenetration come to expression. The expression may rise out of the weakness or undeveloped nature of a body part, as yet, incapable of performing its function. In such moments another body part takes up the responsibility of the dysfunctional or undeveloped limb. As such, it plays either a vicarious role doing what must be done in the absence of the appropriate organ or a modeling role in which something is done that will help the undeveloped part find its own way toward its proper function. (The body metaphor breaks down here and a pedagogical one takes its place.) Thus, Al may decide to organize a prayer and Bible study group in the congregation if Herb's reticence about pietism inhibits him from giving leadership. And Herb may find himself assisting Ken in circulating petitions to city physicians appealing for a nuclear weapons freeze in the hope that Al may catch the vision.

Mutual interpenetration may take place out of strength as well as weakness. Thus a person may have a plenitude of gifts that exceed the boundary of the area of his or her primary ministry. There is a proper permanent place, not just a pioneering and pedagogical role, for a ministry of vitality like that of George sharing his gift and strength with youth. In the same way, a minister of identity, like Herb, is called to share the strength of his gifts of social passion in movements of humanization.

While mutuality means both enrichment and interpretation, it cannot be forgotten that these are movements from points of primary *particular* ministry. The "pastor and teacher" exist to equip the saints for their ministry, not to preempt it. And those called to the church scattered cannot domesticate their gift and claim it in the household of the church gathered. If the particularity of these ministries is neglected, the body is seriously crippled. That particularity is, as we have seen in our reflection on mutuality, not the monopoly by the ministers of identity and vitality of these functions, but their faithful *stewardship* of them. This stewardship entails seeing that the tasks get done by whoever can best do them, not by the stewards' compulsion to perform all of them by themselves. Particular ministry therefore is custodianship of those special ways that keep the body of Christ alive in its vitality and awake in its identity.

The Contexts for Interpreting the Texts of Ministry

The foregoing discussion of the identity and vitality aspects of ministry assumes that there are people within the Christian community primarily responsible for these functions, those traditionally called clergy and laity whom we have designated as ministers of identity and vitality. But the facts of the matter are that (a) those we call clergy and laity are not identified as such in the New Testament (*kleros* does not appear, and *laos* refers to the people of God), (b) there is much more interest in the New Testament in an exploration of the variety of those charged with the identity function and the qualities they need than there is in the definition of clerical offices as such, and (c) there is much more attention to the particular contributions to the body of those with the gifts of vitality than to the definition of an entity, "the laity." Does this not suggest, then, that faithfulness to the Scriptures requires that we abandon the very distinction represented by the words "clergy" and "laity"? Are we not continuing to cripple the laity by perpetuating the distinction between ministries of identity and vitality?

These questions must be seriously confronted by all who take the Scriptures as normative and who are committed to the affirmation of the ministry of the whole people of God. The answer to them drives us beyond the particular issue of ministry to fundamental matters of authority and revelation. What finally determines our theological assertions?

The authority for theological statements here assumed is threefold. The Scriptures of the Old and New Testaments as they witness to Christ and the gospel constitute the *source*, the church and its traditions comprise the *resource*, and contemporary human experience constitutes the *setting* for our views on ministry. Therefore, it is the New Testament perspective on ministry, as it has been in dialogue with the church over two thousand years and is now in conversation with us today, that shapes the position to be taken. This means that the emergence of a pastoral office expressed in different ways and described in different language and its function in the life of the church universal provide the horizon against which we interpret Scripture. The doctrine of ministry, therefore, *develops* from this given as "ever new light breaks forth from God's holy Word." Christian doctrine is enriched as faith learns from and speaks to each new context in which it finds itself. The setting of the world in which we think through our faith and do our mission is the environment in which the resource of tradition and the source book of Christian faith join to answer Bonhoeffer's question, "Who is Jesus Christ for us *today*?"

Our discussion of the ministry issue is the outworking of these authority-revelation assumptions. We take our setting seriously when we respond to the coming-of-age movements

of those formerly treated as dependent, invisible, marginal-
ized nobodies—in our ecclesial context, "the laity." We take
our resource seriously when we relate the new perspectives
to the valid and invalid claims of the tradition—the developed
office of identity and the undeveloped office of vitality. We
take our source seriously when we test the setting, resource,
and perspectives against the biblical norm and source. It is
this method that prompts us to cast the question in terms of
the relation of the pastoral office to a reformulation that challenges its hegemony while retaining its valid functions.

This contextual approach to theological issues—addressing
the Scripture in the light of ecclesial and historical context—
means that in another time with a different set of dynamics
the identity-vitality distinction might not be the most fruitful
category for the exploration of ministry. But for now, both the
hard-won wisdom about the stewardship of identity and the
yet-to-be-won affirmation of the stewardship of the church's
vitalities must find their rightful place in a quest for the ministry of the whole people of God.

The Threefold Office

We have taken the first step toward reenvisioning the continuation of Christ's ministry by seeing that it is the whole
body of Christ and not just a small part of it that is heir to his
work. And we have sought to show how the traditional distinctions of clergy and laity are, in fact, coordinate activities
of this organism which assure its identity and vitality. A deep-
ening of our understanding of who carries forward Christ's
ministry and how that may be done moves us now from our
scriptural inquiry about the body of Christ to an exploration
of a formula from the Christian tradition: the threefold office
of Christ.

We have noted how the doctrine of the threefold office has
directly or indirectly reinforced the idea that those ordained
are the true bearers of Christ's ministry. There is another small
voice in Christian tradition, however, that points in a different
direction. This second scenario of the threefold office of Christ
has its roots in the early centuries. Thus Chrysostom comments on the baptism of the Christian believer: "So also art
thou thyself made king and priest and prophet in the laver.

. . ."[5] The unction associated with baptism in the ancient church was understood as anointing into the threefold office, a practice and formulation noted in the Decree on the Apostolate of the Laity of Vatican II and used today in Roman Catholic rites of Christian initiation.[6] The Reformation gave special accent to this wider concept of the triple office, as stressed in questions 31 and 32 of the Heidelberg Catechism.[7]

While there is this significant expansion of the principle of who and what continues Christ's mediatorial office, its radical implications have yet to be drawn out. Most traditional interpretations stress consideration of personal piety but give no attention to matters of structure and power. These general urgings to "confess his name" (prophet), "present myself a living sacrifice of thankfulness to him" (priest), and "fight against sin and Devil"[8] (king) are expressions of the life of individual piety that have not yet reached the corporate level of ministry in the body of Christ.

Prophetic, priestly, and royal work in Israel were ministry within a covenant community. The threefold work of Christ rose out of the dynamics of the trinitarian life together. Pastoral ministry is exercised within the ecclesial community. The full significance of the threefold office of the ministry of vitality only comes clear when we inquire about its communal function and powers.[9] In doing this, we shall draw a line of precedents that runs from the original models in Judaism of prophet, priest, and king through the transfiguration of these offices in the threefold work of Christ to their present limited articulation in the pastoral ministry.

The Prophetic Office

The prophet brings a word from the Lord. Christ, the prophet, announces the coming of the kingdom. The pastor is called to the pulpit to proclaim the Good News. Prophecy is the power and commission to testify. The form of prophecy is the speaking of the right word at the right time.

The prophetic office of the ministry of the laity, like its antecedents, is the prerogative and command to bear witness to what has been seen and heard. The prophet of vitality tells the Story. But this tale is told fundamentally in the place where this minister of the Word had been called and in a manner befitting that location. The place is "outside the gate of the temple," in the worlds of work, play, family life, the structures of political, social, and economic vitality. And the manner in which the Word is set forth is commensurate with these life worlds and in relationship to the issues that excite and agitate them.

Under the prophetic imperative, the minister of vitality is called to "name the name." But the naming that is fitting in this secular setting is not the uncritical transfer to the secular setting of the code language of the ecclesial community. The task of translation belongs to the ministry outside the gate. As Christ comes to this arena, hidden in the concerns that swarm through the world, so the ministers of vitality are beckoned to keep company with him there and to speak for him and about him in terms of these living issues and in the midst of involvement in them.

The work of evangelism is one of the expressions of the prophetic office speaking the word. But evangelism that takes seriously the secular setting and the incognito Christ (Matthew 25:31-46) names the name and tells the story in the midst of the struggle to make and keep life human. Thus when Bill is asked by business colleagues why he is trying to develop his firm in the way that he is, he not only cites the models of co-management he learned in Harvard Business School, but he also testifies how his faith and his church have helped him to question the worship of the almighty dollar and autocratic views of life and work. As in the apostolic model of engaged evangelism, the deed of healing and hope "indigenizes" the word of truth. Since the prophet is called to name the name in worldly context, that action cannot be either wordless deed or deedless word, but a word in the midst of deed.

The work of apologetics is another form of the prophetic office of the ministers of vitality. Their ministry is among a people who talk in another tongue. Apologetics is the setting forth of the Word in response to the questions put by the people of a given time and place. And so Sandra explains to her colleagues how she differs from fundamentalists on the one hand and atheists on the other in her belief that the first chapter of the Christian story has to do with the "whys and wherefores" of creation—that the good world is brought to existance by and is accountable to God and is not a creation of fate and chance—and not the "how, when, and where," which are subjects appropriate to scientific inquiry.

The prophetic office, as embodied in its antecedents, is one of seeing visions as well as speaking words. The visionary mandate is part of the call to prophecy. What that has meant for Amos and Isaiah, for prophetic clergy, and most of all for the chief prophet, Jesus Christ, is the setting forth of the claims of the vision of shalom. The "things that shall be" call into question the things that are. The collision between God's ultimate future and the world's self-serving agendas for tomorrow results in pain for the visionary in the church scattered. When Fred tells his boss that his commitments to peace will not allow him to work on a missile system that accelerates the arms race and then Fred takes the consequences of that decision, the prophetic voice is being heard on Boston's high-technology Route 128. There is no escape from the world's hostility for those God calls to exercise prophetic ministry.

In the living out of the ministry of the Word and vision, the structures of support and preparation are important: a community that stands by in the moment when the prophetic stance must be taken; equipment with the hard-won theological wisdom that enables a minister of vitality to know the possibilities and limits of historical hope; girding with a spiritual discipline that can save the prophet from self-righteous fury and draw on the grace of Another that finally sustains all ministry. Thus Bill and Sandra and George are supported and their vision is clarified by the life together they have in their Tuesday night group with those who share common history and circumstances. The cost and the joy of prophetic discipleship are made possible and real through these means of grace.

The Priestly Office

The Letter to the Hebrews describes Jesus as high priest who understands the human condition in its weakness and vulnerability, from within the human condition, and who makes sacrifice and supplication to God for us. The pastoral ministry has been viewed as successor to this priesthood in its sacramental celebration, its leadership in prayer and praise, its sharing in the sorrows and bearing the burdens of the people of God.

Long ago the clerical monopoly of this office was challenged by the Reformers. The priestly order is in fact the whole baptized people of God who, for good order, delegate the exercise of its power to its representatives. Sacerdotal delimitation and the polemics of the sixteenth century tended to cause the priestly office of the whole *laos* to be thought of principally in terms of the relocation of the right of access to God from the few to the many. The note of particular responsibility was muted and with it the definition of the priestly role of the church scattered.

Priestly ministers of identity care for the organs of identity in the church gathered: baptism and eucharist through which the birth and nurture of Christian believers take place, the rites that mark the decisive events in the journey of faith, the rhythms of worship. The ministers of vitality carry on a companion work in the institutions in and for which they take responsibility.

The Reformers early saw that this meant the care of souls within the household, as in the "family altar." But the church scatters far beyond residential walls. Ministers of vitality are called to prayer and praise in all the yonder places. Surely this has to do with the life of personal devotion that offers work and play to God. But ministry is much more than individual piety. It entails leadership in community. We are only beginning to understand what this might mean and what forms such "priesting" should take. For example, might there be equivalents in the church scattered to the sacraments of birth and nurture celebrated in the church gathered? Are there peak (or valley) internal experiences in secular institutions that might be liturgically acknowledged and enabled by the ministers of vitality? If a code of ethics developed by Al and his friends wins approval at the next professional society meeting, there will be rejoicing among all in his laboratory. Will Al take his colleagues out to a celebration luncheon that day and maybe offer a prayer of thanksgiving to catch up the feelings of that grateful group?

As with the custodians of identity, so with the stewards of vitality, the priestly office continues the witness of solidarity and vulnerability. Christ, our high priest, bends low to share our maelstrom and miseries. He calls his ministers to join him in his passion. The priestly ministers of vitality bear the burdens of the forlorn and forgotten in those places of living and dying in which Christ has put them. How that ministry is carried out depends on particular gifts given to the priest set there: counselors, listeners, prayers, supporters, helpers, healers, and so on. When Sally comes to Jill with anxiety about the son who has just committed suicide and when even the boss consults Jill about how the results of their company's research can be used overseas, then the work of priesting is not absent from the work place.

How important the task is of identifying the gifts of ministry that the Spirit has distributed throughout the body! Whatever the gift may be that determines the way priesthood is exercised, the office is common to all ministers of vitality. We are co-bearing the burdens assumed by the One present there before us, no stranger to sorrow and acquainted with grief.

The Royal Office

Jesus Christ makes things happen. He defeated the forces of sin, evil, and death on Easter morning and now empowers his purpose in the world, assuring its ultimate victory. When kings were kings, they also made things happen. Thus the victory and power of Christ are described in the classical tradition in regal idiom. And as prophet and priest were anointed, so in Israel the king assumed rulership by the same sign, providing further warrants for the threefold office of Christ, the Anointed One.

While the potency of kings has passed and the masculine image does not do justice to the inclusive rule of Christ, regency does strike the note of *leadership*. Indeed, a different kind of leadership, for here the symbol is broken and remade: Christ reigns from the cross. The victory over the powers and principalities was won through suffering love and continues through vulnerability. This leadership is the power of powerlessness, the potency of servanthood.

The pastoral stewardship of the royal office takes place in the church gathered. When faithful to the crucifixion-resurrection mode of leadership, the pastor is "the servant of the servants of God." Christ came not to be ministered unto but to minister. As Christ called into question the ways of the ancient despot by manifesting leadership through solidarity and suffering, so too the minister of identity lives out the leader role from a position of alongsidedness and serves as a resource and enabler rather than source or Oriental sovereign. Servant leadership is no less leadership. Initiative, ingenuity, and boldness are necessary for the effective equipping of saints for their own work of ministry.

Christ's ministers of vitality are also called to the royal office of initiative, ingenuity, and boldness. In a way this office is the most demanding ministerial role. It is an unambiguous statement of the imperatives of leadership. This royal mandate makes it impossible to view the life of faith in conventional or solitary terms. Leadership requires community; the king needs a kingdom. The institution(s) in which the minister of vitality lives and moves is to that minister what the organized ecclesial community is to the minister of identity. The secular institution exists under the sovereignty of Christ who has called the minister of vitality to give leadership in obedience to that rule of suffering love. And the way in which leadership is exercised is commensurate with the nature of Christ's mode of ruling, as resource and enabler, as servant-leader. When Carl determines in his gracious but firm way that all the doctors in pediatrics should get to see the statistics on burn victims in a 20-megaton bomb holocaust, or when Frank organizes a weekly luncheon meeting with colleagues to think about the moral issues related to genetic manipulation, then there is a royal role of servant leadership being exercised in "the church in this (work) place."

Anxiety about the claims of the ministry of the laity, among laity themselves, is not infrequently related to the burdens of this royal office. While unfamiliar with the theological categories, they intuitively grasp its meaning, sensing the analogy of clerical responsibility in the ecclesiastical setting. They recognize that ministry is far more than the ill defined "being a good Christian," for it demands leadership in the secular context. When this leadership is further clarified in terms of the prophetic and priestly tasks, then this vocation becomes a profound challenge. It is difficult to think of those who choose to walk this way as anything less than heirs to Christ's own ministry.

Conclusion

Why all this talk about the ministry of the laity? There is a gift given and a claim made on Frank and Jill, Paul and Sandra, which places them in direct succession to the ministry of Jesus Christ. Some familiar lines of poetry take on fresh meaning against the backdrop of these questions from the ministry of the whole people of God.

> Christ has no hands on earth but yours
> No feet but yours. . . .

To know that herein lies a charge for the responsibilities of the vital signs and the identifying features of this body is an awesome thought indeed. What if the word were out that all the helpers and healers and risk takers on the Route 128s of this world were gifted and claimed for the prophetic, priestly, and royal ministry that was and is Christ's own work? And what if this act of theological imagination were matched by ways of support, training, accountability, and legitimation by and for these ministries of vitality? We would soon enough be remarking upon the new outpouring of the Spirit in our midst.

Notes

[1] The writer (Gabriel) and the pastor of the congregation (Herb) are members of the group in their capacity as theological resources. The kind of group this is reinforces a central thesis of this essay: at the heart of the ministry of the laity is the ministry of the work place. The latter, however, by no means exhausts the former. Ministry of the whole people of God includes those too young or too old for the work of the world, those whose "work" is neither denominated or remunerated as such, and those who live out their ministry principally in the worlds of leisure and community service/social action. Yet in all these areas it is the life and movement of the body in the world, its vitality, that constitutes the ministry entailed, as does servanthood in the work place. This is also true for those laity for whom the institutional church itself is in an arena of significant ministry. It is carried out there as a ministry of vitality to the extent that the matters of identity uppermost in that place are shaped in the direction of the world.

[2] Quoted in Heinrich Heppe, *Reformed Dogmatics*, rev. and ed. Ernst Bizer (London: George Allen & Unwin Ltd., 1950), pp. 676-677. See also Augustus Strong, *Systematic Theology* (Valley Forge: Judson Press, 1907), pp. 916-

917; and the charge to the minister in almost any Protestant ordination service.

³C. Cronin, "The Sacrament of Order," in George D. Smith, ed., *The Teaching of the Catholic Church: A Summary of Catholic Doctrine* (New York: Macmillan Inc., 1927), pp. 1023-1027.

⁴For example, see Hans-Ruedi Weber, *Salty Christians* (New York: The Seabury Press, 1963), pp. 30-33. The old translation places a comma between "saints" and "for," thereby limiting ministry to apostles, evangelists, pastors, and teachers.

⁵Cited by Hans-Ruedi Weber in "The Spontaneous Missionary Church," *Laity* (November 1957), p. 8. Reprints for Nos. 2-6 (Geneva: Department of the Laity, World Council of Churches, 1962), p. 78. The gathering of important documents as this one in *Laity* and other former publications of the World Council of Churches continues today through *Laity Exchange*, edited by Mark Gibbs of the Audenshaw project. For example, see an update on the thinking of pioneer Hans-Ruedi Weber, "The Battle Is Not Yet Won," *Laity Exchange* (April 1979), no. 6.

⁶"Decree on the Apostolate of the Laity," *The Documents of Vatican II*, ed. Walter M. Abbott, S.J. (New York: Association Press, 1966), p. 491.

⁷*The Heidelberg Catechism* (Philadelphia: Board of Christian Education of the Reformed Church in the United States, 1902), p. 145.

⁸*Ibid.*

⁹Another matter of undrawn conclusions also awaits examination. If ministry entails a call—a personal inner call and an ecclesial outer call—must not the rite of Christian initiation, infant or adult, be followed by a rite of vocational maturity in which the claims of the threefold office made in baptism are accepted in all their personal particularity? So it is with the ordination of the ministers of identity. Can it be otherwise with the ministers of vitality? We leave this derivative question unanswered and concentrate on the nature of the prophetic, priestly, and royal offices conferred upon the entire *laos* in baptism.

IV.

Steps Toward the Future: Putting the Concept to Work

I n this final section the attention shifts from the theological to the practical.

Richard Broholm, in a paper originally composed in the mid-1970s, lays out a group process that was developed to assist laity struggling with institutional change. The process is designed to create picture images that capture the desired goal, drawing forth energy and commitment. The description of the process is set in relation to the work of a historian who analyzes cultures in terms of their images of the future. This, in turn, offers a new perspective on the significance of eschatology. Broholm lays out this material in the hopes of drawing the reader into the work of perfecting the vision-making process in order that it can serve laity who are serious about promoting faithful change.

In a second paper Broholm takes the categories of prophet, priest, and king, which Gabriel Fackre has used, and suggests how they can illuminate the content of the ministry of the laity in very specific terms. He includes, as well, a decision tree for inviting laity to consider the question of whether or not they have a ministry.

In the final paper John Hoffman reviews the agenda of the Laity Project (under whose auspices these papers were developed). He outlines the different angles from which the question of congregational change was approached and reports on the strategies that were actually employed. The strategies are intended to be used, to be adapted and put to work in the ongoing work of reform to which this volume points.

Envisioning and Equipping the Saints for Change

Richard R. Broholm

Where there is no vision, the people perish . . ." (Proverbs 29:18, KJV). "We do not look from the present into the future, but from the future into the present" (Moltmann).

Intent

This essay is an invitation to dialogue. It speaks out of the deep conviction that the time has arrived when the church must earnestly wrestle with its responsibility for the ministry of the laity within secular structures. This responsibility includes the development of a theology of the laity that binds theory and praxis together. Specifically the essay is an attempt to engage the theological community in the task of reworking an envisioning process developed for members of the laity acting as change agents in secular environments.

Approach

This essay will first trace briefly the historical development of the envisioning process, indicating the needs the process was designed to meet and outlining the component steps. It will then relate the process to the seminal historical analysis of the Dutch historian, Frederik Polak. And finally, it will attempt to correlate these insights with the eschatological theology of certain contemporary theologians in order to launch the dialogue necessary for the critique and refinement of the envisioning process.

Context

We are presented with dramatically contrasting visions of the future. A Central Intelligence Agency report released some years ago painted a gloomy picture of global upheavals due to the earth's entrance into a period of adverse weather in which there would be massive crop failures and widespread famine. Simultaneously, Herman Kahn appeared in the daily press, optimistically describing a future of declining population growth, rising levels of affluence, eternal energy sources, and food for everyone.

The explosion of books, articles, and university courses focusing on the future indicates a growing interest, not only among academics but even among average citizens, about where we are headed. The inability of futurologists to reach any consensus may frustrate us, but it has not diminished our preoccupation with the future. Perhaps of greater importance than *what* we envision is *how* we go about envisioning. It is critical to remind ourselves that the futurologist and the theologian approach the future from diametrically opposed methodologies. One scholar points up this contrast by recalling that the predominant methodology of secular futurologists is to anticipate the future by extrapolating present trends or by designing models to meet those trends, while in theology the future confronts and even runs counter to the present, including its developmental trends. The implications of this difference in methodology are highly significant for the way in which the church goes about its task of enabling the ministry of the laity. More will be said about this later. What I wish to underline at this stage of the dialogue is that the question of methodology is not an esoteric issue.

The Development of the Envisioning Process

In 1964, as a result of the vision and leadership of Jitsuo Morikawa, an ecumenical action-research project called Metropolitan Associates was started in Philadelphia to gather data and insights about the church's mission within the secular institutions of a modern metropolis. During the first three years we who were with the project worked closely with over one hundred people from various sectors of the city's life in an effort to understand how the church might equip persons who were committed to the missionary task of calling their work places to the responsible stewardship of institutional resources. Given the complexity and difficulty of this task, we were continually faced with expressions of impotence and fatalism, even from individuals who held significant institutional power. Over the next several years we worked with these persons to help them identify the reasons for their fatalism. Though the issues they faced and the institutions in which they worked were very different, certain common themes began to reappear: they all functioned in lonely isolation with minimal support for their ministry and clearly no visible support group; they found it difficult to work collaboratively with others to effect change; and they lacked a compelling vision of a valued and viable alternative.

Simultaneously with this research effort, we were exposed to and began adapting for support group use a creative problem-solving process called Synectics. This process seemed to have great potential for enabling people of diverse backgrounds and interests to collaborate creatively in solving mutual problems. The Synectics process held promise as a resource for the first two identified needs, enabling the development, within the institution, of a support group whose members could effectively collaborate in overcoming barriers to change. We were still left with the third need: creating vision.

We then were given a grant to work with the Health and Welfare Council in developing a consciousness-raising method for use among the general population, centered on the issues of welfare. Our research led us to the realization that many of the values and beliefs we hold are expressed through images and that these images largely govern our behavior. To change one's behavior involves changing the images that instruct and reinforce that behavior. We found our work and thinking heavily influenced by the writings of Rudolf Arnheim on visual thinking and Kenneth Boulding's distinction between messages and images. Boulding said:

The meaning of a message is the change which it produces in the image.
 When a message hits an image one of three things can happen. In the first place, the image may remain unaffected. If we think of the image as a rather loose structure, something like a mol-

ecule, we may imagine that the message is going straight through without hitting it. . . . [Or the message] may change the image in some rather regular and well-defined way that might be described as simple addition. . . .

There is, however, a third type of change of the image which might be described as a revolutionary change. Sometimes a message hits some sort of nucleus or supporting structure in the image, and the whole thing changes in a quite radical way.[1]

Our critical task, then, became one of enabling people to expose the images that governed their behavior in such a way that incoherences could be examined and alternative messages received. It was at this point that we were highly indebted to Paulo Freire's educational methodology of eliciting people's concern; analyzing their perceptions, values, beliefs, and attitudes; and offering feedback that elicits new responses by bringing to light the problems inherent in their original perceptions.

The method we used was a dialogue process designed to help individuals, in a support-group context, to identify the core images expressing their values and beliefs. By bringing these images to consciousness, we discovered that it was possible for an individual to deal with "messages" (information) that contradicted his or her images (a contradition that the person usually had already experienced at a subconscious level but had rejected). This process of consciousness-raising then made it possible for the individual to choose whether to handle the new "messages" (information) as false or irrelevant. This was a major breakthrough in our thinking! We discovered the vital importance of "positive-vision" images to personal and institutional transformation.

A rather homely illustration of this was stated by a well-known psychologist. In talking about the problem of New Year's resolutions she said that *willpower* is not helpful in changing deeply ingrained behavior patterns because willpower is usually rooted in a negative self-image (e.g., "I'm too fat!" or "I'm too lazy to read a book"). Rather than exerting willpower, a person should hold in mind a positive image of how he or she wants to be. Such an image is much more effective in bringing about change than is willpower.

Over the next several months, by adapting the techniques

of metaphorical excursion from Synectics, we were able to develop the first crude steps in the support-group process called "envisioning." Envisioning is a process of imagining possible futures through the development of visual images that reflect our deepest values and beliefs. The goal of the envisioning process is to enable an individual or an organization to develop a valued vision of the future that is compelling enough to ensure that that person or organization will be able to embody some element of that vision in the present. The envisioning process intends to create new belief structures by giving birth to images that compel actions and break the bonds of assumed limitations.

Four Needs/Concerns that the Envisioning Process Attempts to Address

Because hanging in for long-term, sustained change is difficult, at best, the envisioning process is a helpful tool in dealing with four basic concerns we encountered.

1. *Converting reaction into creative action.* We discovered that unless persons held a positive image of alternative futures, they were left with the negative situation of working *against* that which they experienced as oppressive or intolerable. The envisioning process recognizes the value of the critique (that is, strong images of the negative conditions to be changed). But it became increasingly clear that a sense of oppression was not sufficient, by itself, to enable risk taking or to energize long-term sustained action. True, the negative image does serve as an important launching pad for creative action; but when there is no positive image of the future, persons tended to engage in reactive strategies aimed at annihilating the enemy rather than engaging in strategies for converting the negative situation to a positive one. Envisioning, therefore, includes forming a negative image—but only as a first step in the creative process.

2. *Converting fatalism into hope.* Fatalism is the belief that things cannot change. Creative action depends on hope or a belief in the possibility of a better condition. Imagining desirable futures tends to stimulate a playful, aspiring consciousness. Imagining provides the tool for identifying hope-

ful possibilities in the *present* and a framework from which to organize these possibilities.

3. *Enabling a collaborative rather than a competitive style.* Without a common vision of the future, individuals tend to become locked into competitive efforts, each arguing for his or her way of bringing about change as the "only right way." A common vision gives specific strategies for change a relative rather than an ultimate status. A vision encourages collaboration among different people by highlighting common objectives that can be reached by various means.

4. *Encouraging a "systems" rather than a "problem-solving" approach to change.* An effective solution to one problem is often blocked by the existence of other problems. Several problems can often be traced to the same root condition. To treat a problem in isolation from the larger system of which it is a part is often to contribute, unintentionally, to the creation of a more serious problem than the one persons are attempting to resolve. Peter Drucker, in commenting on this counter-intuitive phenomenon, wrote:

> One thing characterizes all genuine systems, whether they be mechanical like the control of a missile, biological like a tree, or social like the business enterprise: it is interdependence. The whole of a system is not necessarily improved if one particular function or part is improved or made more efficient. In fact, the system may well be damaged thereby, or even destroyed. In some cases the best way to strengthen the system, may be to weaken a part—to make it less precise or less efficient. For what matters in any system is the performance of the whole. . . . [2]

The use of visual imagery in the envisioning process makes it possible to deal simultaneously with several problems in a coherent whole—one picture of the various parts. Often, in so doing, we discover that by relating seemingly divergent problems, we discover a root condition of greater importance, thus enabling the development of a vision that is more comprehensive and more compelling.

The Components of the Envisioning Process

The envisioning process works by helping a person or a group create picture images of conditions as they are now and as they are desired to be in the future. It begins with an analysis of likes and dislikes experienced in the present situation and then uses the identified concerns as the basis for picturing the present as well as wishing for the future. The verbal wishes then become a stimulus for constructing picture images of the vision.

The following is a listing of the steps in the process. (For ease of explanation it will be assumed that we are in a support group in which one individual, the envisioner, is being assisted in developing a vision.)

1. The envisioner is asked to identify his or her *likes* and *dislikes* regarding the situation while the facilitator records these, for the group's benefit, on newsprint. Group members can ask questions, paraphrasing when they are not clear about the data. The envisioner may be asked to give illustrations of specific concerns so that the data provided is as concrete as possible.

2. The group members listen for key image words that seem to capture the situation and then begin to doodle on their notepads until they have produced a picture that they feel captures the critical data. Skill in drawing is irrelevant and often the most valuable images are those that are "artistically" least aesthetic.

3. The facilitator then asks members to redraw their images on large sheets of newsprint. One by one these are presented to the group for its interpretations of what the image is attempting to convey. The facilitator labels specific elements and records the comments and observations of the envisioner. Values, beliefs, and assumptions are noted.

4. Then the envisioner is asked to select that image which best represents his or her situation; this may require redrawing a presented image or having the envisioner draw his or her own image. Again the facilitator makes sure that everyone understands the key elements (likes and dislikes, assumptions, and so on).

5. The facilitator then invites the group and the envisioner to wish, without any concern for what is feasible, for a state or condition that they would see as ideal. Without debate or discussion, these wishes are recorded on newsprint. While this segment of the process is going on, the facilitator again encourages the group members to listen for positive images

and to begin the process of drawing these on their notepads. The participants' aim is to express a visual image that captures both their values and the values of the envisioner.

6. Group members are again asked to redraw these images on newsprint, and one by one the images are examined. It is at this point that differences in values and beliefs are examined and offered by group members to the envisioner without any attempt to be coercive. Considerable consciousness raising occurs at this stage. It is the facilitator's job to protect individuals from manipulation and to maintain a climate in which support and collaboration are encouraged.

7. Again the envisioner is asked either to select the most compelling image, to redraw one, or to create a new one. Values and goals are carefully identified and labeled on the newsprint. When the envisioner chooses a vision image, it can then be used as the basis for analysis and problem solving in order to identify concrete steps that can be taken by the envisioner to begin to embody that vision in the current situation.

Note: The larger process includes problem solving and planning components. A diagram of that process follows, with steps labeled and identified by letter.

A. Likes and dislikes
B. "IS" image
C. Converting concerns into wishes
D. "VISION" image
E. Force field analysis of vision to identify enabling and blocking forces (Force field analysis consists of listing those factors, conditions, and people that are working for and against a given solution or vision.)
F. Problem solving to overcome blocking forces
G. Development of an action plan

Following is an illustration of an "IS" image and a "VISION" image created in a support group of laity change agents for a professor of education in a state college in New York.

Here is a brief interpretation of the "IS" and "VISION" images, indicating their significance for the envisioner:

"IS" image of the classroom
   —High-powered techniques (outboard motor) purport to

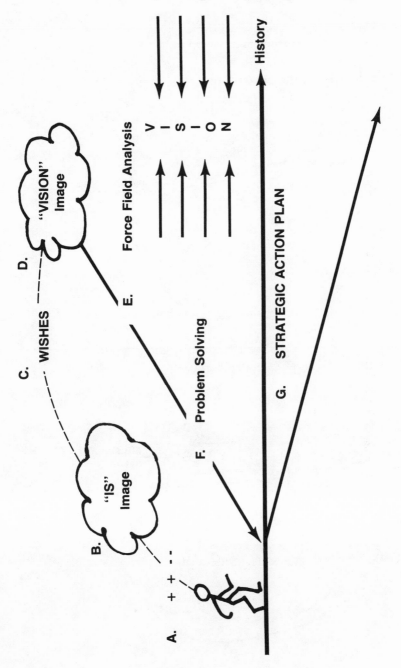

Note: Before reading a brief explanation of these two images, try to interpret their meaning for yourself.

"IS" image of the classroom 1

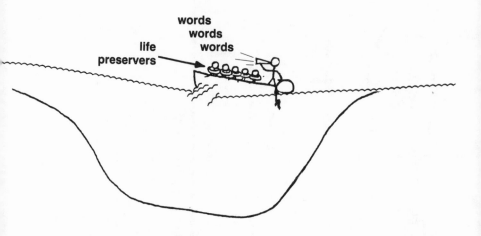

"VISION" image of the classroom 2

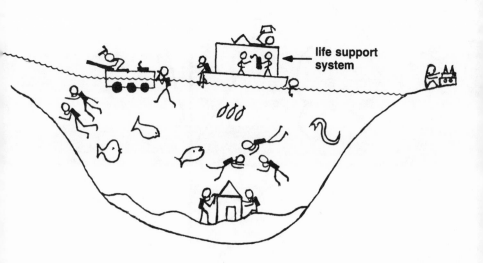

ensure a valid learning environment but allow little opportunity for individuals to move at their own pace.
—Preoccupation with protecting students (life preservers) from risk and failure have attendent problems of conformity and rigidity.
—The classroom (boat) restricts students from exploring their world and discovering insights from first-hand exposure.
—Educational method (life preservers) does not provide students with skills for coping.
—There is a high dependency upon verbal versus visual learning.
—Traditional parental expectations (motor) drive the educational environment, allowing little room for experimentation and divergence.

"VISION" image of the classroom
—Classroom (houseboat) becomes a launching pad for students' learning rather than a restriction against it.
—Key educational resource (life-support system) provides students with the skills necessary to learn and explore on their own.
—The teacher is not readily visible, and could be any one of the figures, which suggests various roles for the teacher (including that of student).
—Students become partners in the teaching process, teaching each other.
—Students are enabled to function at the level of their own readiness (notice the student back on shore building sand castles).
—The learning environment becomes the real world with possibilities of risk and failure but also with support systems (both persons and resources).

The two images provide the potential for a systematic view of education. They can continue to work for the envisioner by raising new questions and possibilities. They provide a visual statement of key values as well as criteria with which to evaluate action plans. The images can be modified or amplified to include new insights.

Envisioning and Social Change in the Theory of Frederik Polak

Two years after the initial work on this process, we came across the work of Frederik Polak, a Dutch historian and sociologist. His work carries profound implications for society at large and, more specifically, for the life and mission of the church in this last quarter of the twentieth century.

Polak is concerned about the relationship between fundamental change in the social order and changes in the dominant images of the future. His writings provide a systematic study of the history of our thinking about the future and the influence that this thought has on the actual course of historical events. His study focuses on Western societies from ancient Greece and Iran through the history of Israel, the Middle Ages, the Renaissance, and finally into the twentieth century.

His thesis is this:

> Any student of the rise and fall of cultures cannot fail to be impressed by the role played in this historical succession by the image of the future. *The rise and fall of images of the future precedes or accompanies the rise and fall of cultures.* As long as a society's image is positive and flourishing, the flower of culture is in full bloom. Once the image begins to decay and lose its vitality, however, the culture does not long survive. The secret of Greek culture, which came to its second flowering in the Renaissance, lies in the imperishable harmony of its image of the future. The endurance of Jewish culture, reborn today in Israel, lies in its fervently held image of the future, which has survived diaspora and pogrom alike. [3]

Polak, near the end of this study, concludes that for the first time in the three-thousand-year history of Western culture we have apparently lost the capacity to create, renew, and renovate our images of the future. Never before has there been such an obvious loss of the will to generate new visions at the same time that utopian images of the future have faded or have been replaced with ambiguous or negative ones.

In analyzing the history of the influence of images of the future on social change, Polak draws some interesting conclusions that are instructive for both our methodological and theological tasks.

1. Social change is a "push-pull process in which a society

is at once pulled forward by its own magnetic images of an idealized future and pushed from behind by its realized past." We stand poised on the dividing line between past and future and thereby become both the bearer and transformer of culture. [4]

2. "Awareness of ideal values is the first step in the conscious creation of images of the future and therefore in the conscious creation of culture, for a value is by definition that which guides toward a 'valued' future. The image of the future reflects and reinforces these values." [5]

3. Images can be thought of as time bombs that explode sometime in the future, although people and societies "who create them have little control over when, where, and how they will explode." [6]

4. Images of the future are elitist in origin in the sense that the "author of the image invariably belongs to the creative minority of a society." [7]

5. "The formation of images of the future depends [on the belief that persons can make a] conscious, voluntary, and responsible choice between alternatives. This means that the development of images of the future and ethics are intimately related." [8]

6. "Thinking about the future requires faith and visionary powers, mixed with philosophic detachment, a rich emotional life, and creative fantasy." [9]

7. "The force that drives the image of the future is only in part rational and intellectual; a much larger part is emotional, aesthetic, and spiritual. . . . It is above all the spiritual nature of the ideals embodied in the image of the future that infuses the image with power." [10]

8. The appeal of the image lies in its picture of a radically different world. ". . . Bold visionary thinking is . . . the prerequisite for effective social change. . . ." Therefore we are not talking about future projections and predictions that are a function of long-range planning but of utopian and eschatological visions that stand in polar contrast to the present. [11]

Polak's study of the future images of Judaism and Christianity is especially significant in light of this last observation about the importance of the vision standing in polar contrast to the present. The prophet's task is to call people to radical conversion based on a radical repentance, to sound the call to a new life of righteousness. It is at this point particularly that Polak, though not a Christian, reads the Scriptures in much the same way as Gutierrez and the liberation theologians. He believes that the prophetic message comes to its fullest flower in the life and teachings of Jesus.

However, in both the Old and New Testaments Polak sees a tendency to spiritualize the message of the prophets and Jesus. Eschatology is otherworldly for Polak, and where he finds strong expressions of it, he feels that the impact of the radical teachings of the prophets and Jesus for social change are diminished. Paul, for example, becomes an antipode to Jesus, and though Polak acknowledges Paul's passion for the kingdom, he contends that Paul sees our role in bringing about the kingdom as essentially passive. This stance "later opened the door for Quietism. The heroic, revolutionary, and utopian ethic [of Jesus] gradually sinks to the level of a comfortable middle-class outlook on life. The utopia of Jesus makes way for the nonworldly eschatology of Christ."[12]

While this understanding of eschatology and Christology appears somewhat naive, from a historian's perspective the history of the church in spiritualizing the gospel would seem to provide ample evidence for Polak's misunderstanding of the creative potential of Christian eschatology for social changes.

Polak concludes with the sober judgment that for both Christians and non-Christians there seems to be little stimulus for discussing the future of the Christian belief-system, though in his judgment this subject is "crucial to the future of Western culture as a whole." He suggests that as theologians attempted to make this belief system more palatable for modern ears by treating one biblical image after another (that is, resurrection, heaven, hell, and others) as mythical in nature, they, in fact, unintentionally, brought about the death of God.

> In the older view of a God who revealed Himself in history, the stream of events in time mirrored God's disposition towards man. The course of history was permeated with divine meaning. . . . Now the evolution of human thought regarding the future has liberated historical time from an intervening superhuman power and leaves it to its own destiny. Time is autonomous, and

the future is no longer determined and directed by a higher hand.

God's removal from history is intimately related to His removal from this world. God has died not only a social death, but also an axiological, ethical, and cultural death. [13]

For Polak, modern theology "has moved from rationalization after the fact to rationalization in advance." In an effort to protect the meaning of the idea of God, theologians have mistakenly believed that God "through being made image-less" can be made more available. But the result has been not only the destruction of the image of God as image but the destruction of the divine image of the future.

Is it still possible that religious images of the future might be revived? There is no reason why this possibility should be excluded in advance, but the chances of such reversal in trend seem fairly limited. Apart from an improbable actual Second Coming . . . there remains the possibility of the future appearance of a new prophetic figure through whom God would speak and give . . . a new religious image of the future. The more Christianity is mechanized and the God-consciousness of men minimized in accordance with the spirit of the times, the less chance there is of successfully giving a new content and form to eternal truth as an adequate and timely answer to the challenge of the future. A new prophet would not be crucified; he would simply be ignored or laughed at. [14]

Polak then briefly explores the possibility that some equivalent faith, such as Neo-Buddhism, evolutionary vitalism, humanism, a religious syncretism might be able to replace the role of Christianity in providing us with positive visions of the future. But in the final paragraph he returns almost plaintively to assert:

We do not know. But one thing must not be forgotten: if the present trends of thought prove capable of destroying Christianity, not only as a social institution but also spiritually in and through its own adherents, then there will remain little hope for substitute currents of a religious or cultural nature. All the structurally related and associated expressions of Western culture are equally threatened; the total pattern of culture is at stake. [15]

The implications of the thinking of Frederik Polak for our work in enabling the ministry of the laity in institutional change are several. Clearly his study about the role of positive images of the future on social change confirms many of our own observations even though his work is focused on larger social and cultural phenomena. In addition, the validity of specific steps in the envisioning process is underlined and reinforced by his theory.

Perhaps the most important implications are those that are directed at the theological task related to the process of envisioning, and it is to these that we turn in the last section of this essay.

Christian Eschatology and the Process of Envisioning the Future

Polak presents an imposing challenge to the Christian community. If visionary images are critical to a society's ability to grow toward more just and humane ends and if our own heritage is richly endowed with utopian images of the kingdom that speak of hope, then our failure to embody that vision may well be the basis for God's most wrathful judgment. The arresting question that confronts us out of Polak's study is: Can we who bear the name Christian once again be stirred to define and clarify those images of the kingdom in such a way that they speak with power to a world grown sick with pessimism and despair? Do we have the courage and the will to discover how those images of the kingdom can be meaningfully embodied, both personally and institutionally, so that once again they become the time bombs whose explosive power breaks us away from the grip of a dying culture?

As already stated, the intent of this essay is to attempt to lay the groundwork for an interdisciplinary, integrative effort that seeks to link theory (theology) and practice in such a way that it makes the rich resources of our faith available to the laity who bring competence and commitment to their ministry in the world.

The envisioning process is a rough and imperfect tool that has already proven its usefulness in helping persons develop positive images of the future that enabled them to begin the risky pilgrimage of personal and organizational change. But there are significant gaps and weaknesses; the most serious, in my judgment, is the lack of a clear and self-conscious method of drawing on our biblical and theological heritage.

The work of certain theologians of hope holds great promise. But where do we begin the dialogue? Following are likely starting points.

1. *The problem of authority for the vision.* More than once we experienced the phenomenon of change agents creating positive, alternative visions of the future that seemed to embody a compelling sense of the gospel. However, because the connecting link to the tradition was not obvious, the change agents seemed to lose nerve and conviction. How can we self-consciously use the Bible and our theology to help us critique our current situation (the "IS" image) and inform our images of the future (the "VISION" image)? Does this mean we need to address the Scriptures in terms of the images they present and recast these other images in visual pictures that might more effectively put them at our disposal?

The problem of authority may be a deeper one than that of the self-conscious identification and classification of biblical images. It may go to the questions of just exactly what is the Christian faith, in what is it centered, and, hence, how is its enactment to be creditable?

What then constitutes the hard core of the Christian faith, and how can laity lay hold of this without spending four or more years in seminary? Strategically, I would submit that a critical starting point would be to engage members of the laity in wrestling with biblical theology and the questions of authority at the place of members' highest self-interest: their vision for themselves and the organizations that claim so much of their time and energy.

2. *The problem of connecting the ultimate vision with the penultimate reality.* Polak insists, and our own experience would support the thesis, that one's vision of the future needs to stand in radical polarity to the present if it is to exert a strong pulling force; and yet this distance between the "IS" and "VISION" can also lead to a feeling of impossibility before we have begun. Ken Cauthen, professor of theology at Colgate Rochester, in an unpublished article, affirms the importance of this tension when he writes:

> The concept of the kingdom of God needs to be translated into contemporary terms which preserve the tension between immanent historical possibility (Thy Kingdom come on earth) and

transcendent ultimate perfection (as it is in heaven). Without the former a vision cannot be recognized as concretely relevant for its time. Without the latter ideals do not stand out sufficiently beyond the ambiguities of the present to serve either as a judgment on historical actuality or as a lure for future realization.

Polak may be on the wrong track, with his inadequate understanding of eschatology. A more adequate approach builds on Bonhoeffer's Christology: "Now the living Lord appears to us as the *eschatos*, the Last One; he comes to meet us out of the future." [16]

Pannenberg, in his conviction of the priority of the future, also underlines this approach to Jesus' message of the immanent kingdom when he insists that the present is not independent from the future:

Rather does the future have an imperative claim upon the present, alerting all men to the urgency and exclusiveness of seeking first the Kingdom of God. As this message is proclaimed and accepted, God's rule is present and we can even now glimpse his future glory. In this way we see the present as an effect *of* the future, in contrast to the conventional assumption that past and present are the cause of the future. . . . With Jesus the eschatological hope itself became the only source of knowledge and guide for living. [17]

Each of these theologians seems to be pointing us, not to the wrenching pain of an impossible tension between the now and the not yet, but rather to that experience of liberation and celebration that comes from the effective integration of personal piety and active engagement with God's mission of shalom. Richard Neuhaus in his introduction to *Theology and the Kingdom of God* moves us in that direction.

The dynamic of Christian piety is the yearning for what is to be, not gratitude for past forgiveness. . . . The kind of Christian engagement in social change that has staying power because it is rooted in Christian piety is that of the martyred Martin Luther King: "I have seen the promised land. I may not get there with you. But it doesn't matter now. We as a people will get to the promised land. My eyes have seen the glory of the coming of the Lord!" [18]

If this is one fruitful avenue of approach to holding in tension the ultimate vision and the penultimate reality, then we have our work cut out for us. For traditional piety has not helped us to identify Christ coming to us out of his future into a meeting in our marketplace. Our sight has been dimmed to his reality in the midst of our daily offering, and we will have to discover how and where he is meeting us and to what he is calling us. Can this happen as we meet in a supportive community with other Christians and attempt to envision that future which Christ calls us to embody today? I would like to believe so.

3. *The problem of envisioning as an upper-class activity out of touch with the awesome character of unrelenting evil.* Here we have several related yet distinct problems: the elitist nature of envisioning (already acknowledged by Polak); the difficulty of simultaneously dealing with hope and defeat; the theological problem of evil; and the question of whether those who have carefully insulated themselves from suffering can effectively create positive visions that are compelling and authentic for those who suffer.

In one of his books, Moltmann insists, "There is not true theology of hope which is not first of all a theology of the cross."[19] He then proceeds to recite a history of the end of optimism by reminding us of Auschwitz and Vietnam and finally of the fact that for those of us who are white, rich, and dominant, a theology of hope must emerge out of the cries of those who starve and those who are oppressed.

This calls us to remember the words of Bonhoeffer in one of his last letters from prison in which he pleads for an understanding of Christian worldliness as a participation in the sufferings of God in the world.

> Man's religiosity makes him look in his distress to the power of God in the world. . . . The Bible directs man to God's powerlessness and suffering; only the suffering God can help. . . . [This] opens up a way of seeing the God of the Bible, who wins power and space in the world by his weakness. . . . Man is summoned to share in God's sufferings at the hands of a godless world.
>
> He must therefore really live in the godless world without attempting to gloss over or explain its ungodliness in some religious way or other. He must live a 'secular' life, and thereby share in God's sufferings.[20]

May it not be true that there is an authentic dialectic between the capacity to envision positive visions of the future and also to experience the profundity of human suffering in the present? In fact, may it really be that our visions of the future will be powerless, vapid, and apathetic unless they emerge out of a genuine identification with the reality of evil (in the "IS" image) and a participation in the sufferings of God in the world? When and if this happens, envisioning might be no longer an elitist activity but fundamentally an expression of our oneness in Jesus Christ and our solidarity with all humankind.

Notes

[1] Kenneth E. Boulding, *The Image* (Ann Arbor, Mich.: The University of Michigan Press, 1956), pp. 7-8.

[2] Peter Drucker, S.E.W.R.P.C. newsletter (1963) quoted in "A Systems Approach to Management."

[3] Frederik Polak, *The Image of the Future*, trans. Elise Boulding (New York: Elsevier Scientific Publishing Co., 1973), p. 19.

[4] *Ibid.*, p. 1.

[5] *Ibid.*, p. 10.

[6] *Ibid.*

[7] *Ibid.*, p. 13.

[8] *Ibid.*

[9] *Ibid.*, p. 22.

[10] *Ibid.*, pp. 13-14.

[11] *Ibid.*, p. 22, *et passim.*

[12] *Ibid.*, p. 56.

[13] *Ibid.*, p. 234.

[14] *Ibid.*, pp. 235-236.

[15] *Ibid.*, p. 236.

[16] Dietrich Bonhoeffer, *No Rusty Swords* (New York: Harper & Row, Publishers, Inc., 1970), p. 302. Quoted in Franz J. van Beeck, S.J., "Küng's *Christ Sein*: A Review Article," *Andover Newton Quarterly* (March 1976), p. 281.

[17] Wolfhart Pannenberg, *Theology and the Kingdom of God*, ed. Richard Neuhaus (Philadelphia: The Westminster Press, 1969), p. 54.

[18] Richard Neuhaus, "Wolfhart Pannenberg: Profile of a Theologian," in Pannenberg, *Theology and the Kingdom of God*, pp. 40-41.

[19] Jurgen Moltmann, *The Theology of Hope* (New York: Harper & Row, Publishers, Inc. 1976), p. xv.

[20] Dietrich Bonhoeffer, *Letters and Papers from Prison*, ed. Eberhard Bethge (London: SCM Press Ltd., 1953, 1967, 1971, rev. and enlarged ed. New York: Macmillan Inc., 1972), p. 361.

Toward Claiming and Identifying Our Ministry in the Work Place*

Richard R. Broholm

Today the church is beginning to come to the truth that the ministry of the laity is not limited to the ministries men and women perform as church school teachers, board and committee members, and assistants in worship. We are being encouraged to discover that ministry is also related to our workday roles as tool and die makers, nurses, public school teachers, accountants, bank managers, and home-makers. We are being asked to think of our faith, not simply as a part-time affair focused largely on what we do within the gathered Christian community, but also as the fundamental way we experience and incarnate what we believe about God and God's world in the whole round of daily activities, including what we commonly refer to as our work place.

There is good reason to celebrate the growing willingness of the institutional church to affirm the full ministry of all God's people! Nevertheless, the task of actually claiming and identifying our ministry in the work place is, for most of us, exceedingly difficult.

The purpose of this essay, therefore, is to propose a method for differentiating various types or forms of Christian ministry so that we can see more clearly how we can and do incarnate Christ's ministry in our daily lives, particularly in the work place.

The ideas expressed in this essay reflect the work and think-

*I wish to give special thanks to the invaluable contributions and suggestions to this essay made by three of my colleagues: Mimi Bonz, John Hoffman, and Dave Specht.

ing of two task forces that have met over the last three years as part of the Andover Newton Laity Project. Using a variety of approaches, these task forces have conducted action research on the experiences of Christian laity engaged in ministry in their work places. Our work to date has led us to several underlying theological assumptions and two observations that seem important to share as a preface to the basic content of this essay.

Briefly, our theological assumptions are:

1. All ministry is Christ's ministry.

2. All Christians are called to incarnate this ministry in all the arenas of their lives.

3. There is no arena, however demonic, to which one cannot be called by God to minister.

4. Christ's ministry is one of reconciling all things to God. This ministry of reconciliation brings healing and wholeness not only to and between persons but also to the whole created order.

5. Those who self-consciously acknowledge Christ's lordship over their lives experience the empowerment and support of the Holy Spirit in ways that add depth, power, and discernment to their ministry.

6. Christians are not alone in participating in Christ's ministry. Those who do not consciously bear the name of Christ may also share in his ministry. Thus, one task of the Christian is to recognize, affirm, and celebrate Christ's reconciling action in others.

7. Christ's ministry is incarnated in very diverse functions and reflects a wide variety of gifts, but there is no hierarchy of value; no ministry is worth more than any other.

8. Christ's ministry is to persons *and* structures.

9. Organizational structures and processes can incarnate Christian values and thus can be instruments of ministry. They can serve to support, affirm, and encourage individuals whether or not those persons see what they do as ministry. (An example of this is the management process of performance review. When rooted in a commitment to enable each person to claim and use their unique talents, performance review can be an instrument by which persons discover a sense of self-worth and direction in their lives.)

In light of these assumptions, we have been informed by two observations. First, in our attempt to redress the current imbalance within the church in which "lay ministry" refers only to what we do with the margins of our time and energy in what is commonly referred to as "church work," we believe it would be a grave error now to focus exclusively on ministry outside the institutional church. Christ's ministry is one. Though it manifests itself through us in many diverse ways and utilizes a vast variety of gifts, we need to see it as an interdependent whole. By gaining insight and clarity about the ministry of administration as performed by a branch bank manager, we may also come to new insight about the nature and content of the ministry of a parish pastor or a seminary dean. Thus, while we need to pursue the specific nature of each individual's ministry—if our insights are to be both faithful and empowering—we must not overlook the reality that all ministries are inextricably linked together and therefore inform and enrich one another.

Second, our experience is that most Christians are not at all eager to have everything they do "baptized" as ministry. There is too much pain and ambiguity around our work to have it glibly labeled as Christ's ministry. Both integrity and the desire for empowerment and affirmation call for more careful discrimination and discernment. Therefore, though there are obvious problems in attempting to define and describe what constitutes Christ's ministry, the risks are worth the effort since to leave Christians with the existing lack of distinctions is truly disabling.

Differentiating Types of Ministry

In attempting to gain new clarity about the nature and content of Christ's ministry in and through us in the complete round of our daily lives, one approach that seems to hold genuine promise is to look at what we do in terms of the threefold office of Christ's ministry as priest, prophet, and king. While traditionally this interpretation of Christ's ministry has been used only to address the nature and content of the ministry of clergy, we believe that it can be a source of illumination in thinking about the full ministry of Christ's body.

In the following pages these three interrelated functions are further divided into nine types of ministry under which a vast variety of diverse and sophisticated forms of ministry can be categorized. Let us examine how the three roles of priest, prophet, and king and their various subroles might be expressed and lived out in today's world.

Priest

The *priestly* or *pastoral ministry* of Christ's body, according to our typology, involves three major functions: *modeling, caring, celebrating.*

Modeling

This form of ministry refers to the personal behavior of the minister, how in our being and acting we testify to a new creation breaking forth. Often the personal behavior code for Christians has reflected a negative view of the world. Christians don't smoke, drink, or dance. While we may smile at these examples that mark a particular kind of Christian piety, we should remind ourselves that they are rooted in an attempt to reflect the biblical admonition not to be conformed to this world.

Modeling as a form of ministry encompasses both the refusal to act in certain ways (e.g., taking bribes, bearing false witness against another, demeaning another through word or glance, or using of racist or sexist language) and the decision to adopt alternative behaviors. Today the conscious decision to simplify one's life-style and to reduce the consumption of energy are examples of modeling a new reality in Christ.

Modeling, therefore, is essentially a ministry of incarnation. It involves witnessing to the presence of God's kingdom through living our lives as though we were first and foremost its citizens. The ministry of modeling includes making that new reality a genuine possibility today. By living out a new reality, we offer the hope of change to others in their own lives.

Modeling also includes the conscious identification of our gifts or talents and their careful stewardship by using those gifts that we have where we are called, and, equally, by saying no to requests that lie beyond our gifts or our call. Modeling also includes a conscious desire to be faithful stewards of the resources and gifts that God has entrusted to our care.

Caring

The second expression of a priestly or pastoral ministry comes to visibility in how we care for the needy and the oppressed. It is rooted in the conviction that one finds one's life in losing it in service to others. Caring for the invalid neighbor or child, listening to the bereaved friend or co-worker, providing a house for the homeless, or visiting the sick and imprisoned are traditional ways we have understood this form of ministry. What we have often failed to see is that the contractor who builds houses, the lab technician who tests for cancer, and the postal worker who bridges the gap between distant friends are all engaged in a caring ministry even though it is unlikely they will ever intimately know the persons they serve.

How these ministries are performed may be a more crucial test of whether they are incarnations of Christ's ministry than what our intentions are. For example, the lab technician's ministry in contributing to a helpful and timely diagnosis is finally more dependent on the care given to ensuring accuracy in the tests than in the compassionate feeling the technician has for the sick.

We are called to understand and act on the conditions that led to the oppression, whether the oppression be the plight of starving children, friends struggling with destructive relationships filled with anger and bitterness, co-workers trapped in dead-end jobs, or whole communities held hostage by systems or traditions that impoverish or terrorize. (Seeking knowledge about the sources of oppression is an important aspect of faithful ministry.) Caring requires that we work for change.

Celebrating

The ministry of celebrating is that of recognizing and calling attention to the truth of God's presence and the in-breaking of God's kingdom in our everyday affairs. This may include celebrating the newly identified and claimed gifts of our co-workers, discerning and affirming moments of grace or the discovery of a new sense of call, and remembering past events in which others experienced the liberating truth of God's love.

While it seems clear how celebration is meted out by clergy and those charged with leading Christian liturgy, how it takes place in the secular work place is less obvious. Part of the reason for this confusion may be rooted in the fact that our Sunday liturgy fails to make clear the connections between our work and our worship (Romans 12). If the drama of our salvation does, in fact, speak of God's reconciling action in every facet of our lives, then our liturgical reenactment of this fact should enable us to see clearly the linkage.

One potential illustration of celebrating occurred in the executive office of a manufacturer of office products. The company, after several successes in the development of new products, finally produced—at considerable cost—a product that dramatically bombed. The losses to the company were so profound that for months the senior officers were immobilized. Finally, the president gathered them together in his office. In the center of the office was a wooden casket. Solemnly he placed the offending piece of equipment in the casket, read a brief liturgy acknowledging its "death," and then proceeded to bury the "departed" in a grave dug behind the plant. Remarkably, but quite understandably, the company officers were finally able to lay to rest this albatross that had haunted them for months and get on with the business of serving their customers and employees. The truth of the Christian doctrine of death and resurrection had, at some level, been dramatically experienced and celebrated in the context of the work place. Linking the undergirding truths of our faith with the dynamics of our work places is essential.

Prophet

The *prophetic ministry* of Christ's body is reflected in this typology by three major functions or types of service: *teaching, critiquing,* and *envisioning.*

Teaching

There is a certain obviousness about this form of ministry that may prevent us from probing more deeply the impact it may have. Knowledge is power, and when knowledge is held as the prerogative of a privileged or special class, it can be a tool for keeping others in servitude. The specialized language systems of most disciplines often are used (whether intentionally or not) as a means of denying power to some (e.g., persons usually referred to as "lay" whether it be in the medical, legal, or theological disciplines). Providing information, ideas, skills, or ways of viewing reality can be profoundly empowering for people when it is done so as to foster competence and potency.

One who teaches or shares knowledge so as to empower another is engaged in ministry. This may be done in the formal context of the classroom or in the factory where a worker explains how to run a machine to a new employee. It can occur as my physical therapist helps me to understand my body and its needs and shows me how to become more proactive in the healing process. Teaching may be incarnated in the mother of grown children whose sage counsel about parenting helps a young father find freedom to be a host to his children, accepting them as gifts from God to be stewarded rather than manufactured products of his own ego.

Critiquing

Critiquing is the prophetic function of challenging the existing order. It is more than imparting information or ideas that empower. Critiquing is rooted in the conviction that the existing way of perceiving reality is wrong! Such understandings of reality are not readily apparent or easily followed because of prevailing assumptions about what is "true" or "possible." Luther, in his struggle with his own conscience and his careful reading of Scripture, finally came to the painful conclusion that his church's doctrine and practice simply were wrong! When I worked for Hay Associates—the Cadillac of compensation consultants—I came to believe that its sophisticated compensation evaluation process, which had originally been rooted in a concern for justice (e.g., "internal equity"), now reflected a concern for external competitiveness. The discrepancy in wages between salaried and hourly rated people was simply accepted. Raising this concern is an example of critiquing. Corporations, government agencies, even church institutions, often shun the "whistle-blower" who publicly calls into question prevailing norms and practices. Therefore, this form of ministry needs great support and encouragement by the Christian community lest the minister lose courage or perspective.

The prophet or critic ministers by challenging the existing order, but having no vision or suggestion of alternative options, the ministry is often incomplete.

Envisioning

The gift to see beyond the present reality to what is "really real" or ultimately true is a critical component of prophetic ministry. Implicit in every challenge to the existing order is a different set of values or a hope or dream about what might be. But many prophets are unable to speak as clearly about the new option as they are to discern the failure of the old. One of the reasons for my own failure at Hay was that I was not equipped to provide a compelling alternative for a more just compensation process that could be put into practice. Envisioning is providing a clear and compelling articulation of an alternative option that has the capacity to free us from our fears and draw us toward an unknown future.

The envisioner can be a corporate planner who questions existing assumptions and opens up as yet unthought-of possibilities. Sometimes this occurs by simply putting on different "image spectacles" and seeing the current reality from a totally fresh vantage point. An example in the computer industry was IBM's shift from thinking of itself as a manufacturer of calculating machines to being in the information business. At a different level is the envisioner who sees in the prostitute a person of great worth and intrinsic value. Don Quixote's vision of Dulcinea became the vehicle for her transformation. In this sense "having a vision is perceiving reality." It is not only hoping for what might be, but actually having the discerning wisdom to see in someone what is true.

I believe the ministry of evangelism (i.e., sharing the Good News of God's love incarnate in Jesus Christ) can be understood as significantly combining all three: teaching, critiquing, and envisioning.

King

The *kingly* or *administrative ministry* of Christ's body is incarnated in these three major subheadings: *making and distributing, managing,* and *building.*

Making and Distributing

Ministry is not limited to how we relate on a one-to-one basis with other persons but is also incarnated in how we relate to the created order itself. Our faithfulness as stewards of God's creation is profoundly reflected in how we use our natural resources.

What we produce and how we use what we produce is a basic statement about who we worship. Saying this does not mean that we have great clarity about what constitutes ministry in this category. For example, while it would seem obvious that the process of creating wool, cloth, and finally a coat is a form of ministry that provides warmth for persons, it is harder to see how the designer of high fashion clothes is engaged in Christ's ministry.

Ministry is performed in how and what we manufacture and also in how the product is distributed. The ministry of the farmer in producing food to feed people seems clearly affirmed by Christ when he "ordains" us to feed the hungry. However, if the way we distribute food allows some to overindulge and others to go without, then the ministry of distribution is sinfully performed. This category of ministry is a striking example of how structures, systems, and processes are instruments of ministry and, therefore, how those who establish policy and manage the production and flow of goods and services are potentially Christ's ministers.

Managing

Those who manage organizations and systems and, therefore, also persons and information clearly affect the shape and health of God's created order. The pollution of the environment, the maintenance of hazardous work environments, and the unequal distribution of essential goods are but three examples of ministry that have been unfaithfully conceived and performed.

The Christian minister who is called to a ministry of management is, by the very nature of the gift, called to a ministry of stewarding the gifts of God's creation. This involves, as the former category suggests, managing the processes of production as well as stewarding the gifts and talents of persons. The manager who sees in her employees not only the "means of production" but also persons whose God-given talents are to be evoked, nurtured, and employed in meaningful labor is one who understands, at some level, the kingly ministry of Christ.

Evoking and encouraging the faithful use of the gifts of others, whether done by a supervisor or a co-worker or fellow parishioner, is a ministry of management in which the person exercising the ministry is an instrument of God's reconciling *and* liberating action in Jesus Christ.

Building

This last category of ministry is the least clear and most intriguing of all. While the very word "building" might readily be seen to apply to a ministry of physical construction like that of Nehemiah's rebuilding of Jerusalem, it would be superficial not to recognize also the relationship between the building of physical structures and the building of community. From a careful reading of the book of Nehemiah, it would seem evident that Nehemiah's concern was more for the reestablishment of a community of faith than for the reestablishment of a wall and some buildings. Yet the vehicle for accomplishing the former was inextricably linked with his talent for accomplishing the latter. May the creation of a corporation or a hospital or a school, itself, be an exercise of Christ's ministry?

A related approach to this category is evident when we talk about the ministry of building up Christ's body within an organizational structure. We think we have some clear understanding of what this means in a church organization like a local congregation, but what does it mean to "build up" Christ's body within Hay Associates? Are only Christians to be a part of the building up, or is the concept more universal, and, if so, in what way can we speak of it as Christ's body?

Just as pastors have a crucial role in shaping this type of ministry within a congregation, so do certain gifted men and women in secular organizations. But what does Christian liturgy and Christian tradition mean in this very different context in which the institution does not think of itself as being a steward of God's creation?

While it may be disconcerting to conclude with a series of questions, it is an accurate reflection of where we are in this enterprise of trying to bring new insight and clarity to our ministries in God's world. We have many more questions than answers. Our work and thinking reflected here form a call to others to engage the questions and to share in the task of developing an inclusive theology of ministry that speaks to the *whole* ministry of *all* God's people.

NOTE:

The attached typology has been designed as a "decision tree"; that is, it is an attempt to trace the possible responses to and implications of the question "Do you have a ministry in the work place?"

For example, if a person said yes to this question, then he or she would proceed to the top of the chart to discern what is the nature and content of the particular ministry, selecting from one of the nine different options. If, however, the person said "No," that response might be like the first one recorded: "Ministry is what clergy do, and anyway I've never had a call."

In an effort to help persons who feel this way examine a larger vision of ministry and see and discern ways in which God might be calling them, a local congregation could draw on resources and strategies to deepen persons' spiritual formation and raise their consciousness about the *full* ministry of *all* God's people. If the response was similar to "It's a great vision, but frankly it is too threatening to go it alone," the persons could be invited to share in small groups that meet regularly for mutual support and encouragement.

The decision tree is designed to chart the several responses that can be given to the question "Do you have a ministry in the work place?" indicating possible areas to be researched and pointing to new ways of conceiving the rich breadth of options in ministry.

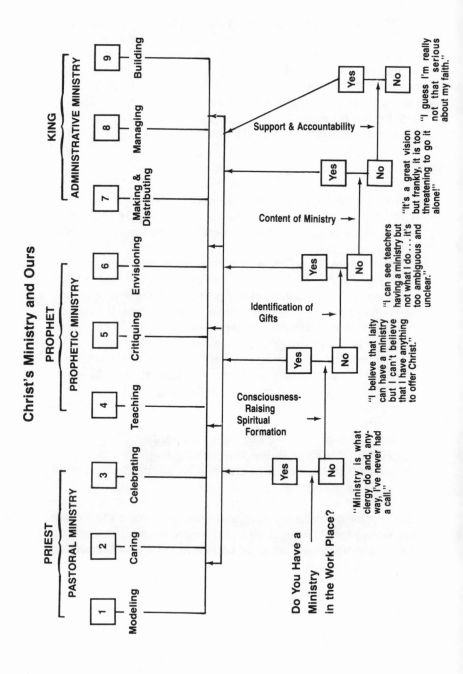

Making a Start: Strategies for Change in the Local Congregation

John S. Hoffman

A single vision, sometimes differently interpreted, has been illuminating these essays. This vision sees the church as one body, the body of Christ, a body made up of many members, in which each and every member is engaged in full-time ministry. This vision assumes that for most members of the body, this full-time engagement will coincide with their secular work places. The vision assumes that the primary role of the local congregation is to equip the laity for these ministries in the world.

Few of us can say that this vision is embraced, explicitly, by our congregations. Fewer still can say that it has really been put into practice. But while we lack complete models, work has begun. Building on the foundations of earlier efforts, the Andover Newton Laity Project came into being in 1977. It was designed to draw together the institutions in the church system—seminary, denomination, and congregation—to see how these institutions might change if they were to manifest the vision.

Three denominations, the Andover Newton Theological School, and six local congregations agreed to enter into covenant with one another for five years to experiment with change. When those participants first came together, they examined the vision and then analyzed what stood in the way of its realization. From that analysis emerged an agenda that constituted the focus of the laity project.

Agenda for Change

What was that agenda, and how can it be acted upon in a local congregation?

1. Consciousness Raising

The starting point for change is the recognition that something is wrong. But the incentive for change, its motive power, is more likely to flow from a sense of new possibilities, from a vision of transformation. The work of consciousness raising needs to move back and forth between these twin dynamics of the need for change and the vision of change.

Discerning what's wrong may be complex. Because the vision, especially as it includes the work place, is not prevalent, there are not many laity who are consciously frustrated about not being supported for their ministry in their daily work. There may be a few. But more likely there are many who feel vaguely dissatisfied, who feel the church is cut off from the other sectors of their lives, who feel the maintenance work of the congregation as only tangentially related to faith, who yearn for some more profound integration, who suffer with a sense that their faith is less than it might be and their work less meaningful than it might be. In addition to these people, who represent a positive force in the change process, there will be others who are content, more or less, with the way things are.

Given the complexity of the problem, how can a congregation begin the work of consciousness raising? The initial step that we took in the project was to invite each congregation to form a core group of three people, a pastor and two members of the laity, at least one of whom had some sense of ministry in his or her work place. Later we expanded the groups to five or six members. The significance of beginning with a group is threefold. First, it offers a base of support for what is inevitably a long process. Second, it provides a core of people who can experiment with each other in identifying and supporting each other's ministries. Third, it represents, in miniature, a model of what the embodied vision looks like. In launching an effort for change, probably no step is more important that the discerning and calling together of a group that can incarnate and pastor the change process. The specific kinds of strategies which such a group might implement are suggested in the items that follow.

A question that bears comment at the outset is the role of the pastor. Our group began with the pastor. Is it necessary to include him or her? It may seem contradictory in pursuing the ministry of the laity to accentuate the role of the clergy, but in fact we believe it is very much in line with our faith in body life. The emphasis on the ministry of the laity is not an attempt to denigrate the life of the church or the work of the clergy. It is rather an attempt to reset that life in a broader context, namely, the service of the world. The church as institution is essential to this effort. The role of clergy is a vital one in this vision. And pragmatically, while individuals within the congregation can certainly move to support one another and to encourage one another in ministry, organizational change is virtually impossible without the committed participation of clergy.

2. Gifts and Call

Paul tells us that the members of the body are gifted for ministry. But the fact is that few of us can name our gifts. Our contention is that giftedness includes not only the church-centered skills that we have traditionally identified—preaching, teaching, healing, and the like—but also the talents that we are individually graced with at birth and through the growing-up process. These inherent and acquired abilities are what we have to serve with, what we have to offer God. The more we are clear about our gifts, the more we are able to recognize a call, since often calls come in response to how others perceive our gifts. Our own clarity enables us to respond to calls for which we really are gifted and to refuse those for which we do not have the requisite gifts. This process is as critical in our secular work as in our roles within the gathered community.

One way of beginning to focus attention on this issue is to invite the nominating committee to be more intentional about what gifts a given position within the church requires and what gifts nominated individuals possess. Nominating committees can also take more seriously the process of extending a call, including taking responsibility to see that individuals refuse calls that are not appropriate. The fact of having the necessary gifts does not itself signify that the call is right. A person's overall pattern of commitments as well as available time and energy are also critical. A nominating committee can set a new tone by making it clear to church members not only that the committee is interested in helping them consider whether a given position might be right for them, but also that the committee is ready to celebrate a refusal when that refusal represents the members' clarification and claiming of other responsibilities.

As well as working with a nominating committee, the core group members can also begin the process of identifying each other's gifts. [1] The core group, once it has familiarity with a process, can encourage other groups within the church to do the same. The attention to gifts has enormous carry-over in other areas—with our families, our children, and in the work place. The focus reminds us of the stewardship of our own gifts and the importance of recognizing and developing the gifts of others.

3. Support and Accountability

One key feature of the body is that the members have *different* gifts. We do not all do the same things well; no one of us does all things well. We need one another. This mutual need is born out of our life together in which our complementary talents are necessary for the accomplishing of a wide variety of tasks.

A second dimension of support, enhanced by this first reality, happens in coming together to reflect on the work that we do individually. When we gather as the congregation, we do so as individuals who have primary responsibilities in other arenas, often responsibilities about which our fellow members know little or nothing. As we come to regard these secular arenas as opportunities for ministry and as we begin to engage in ministry, we become increasingly needful of support—emotional support to help us endure and strategic support to help us to be wise. Despite our unfamiliarity with each other's vocational spheres, we can provide powerful support, in part because of the reality of our being differently gifted.

Within the laity project one of our major focuses was on the establishment of support groups. These groups, of five or six people, would meet weekly for two hours to hear about each other's ministries. The meetings would begin with a few minutes for centering, consisting of Scripture reading or prayer, and then proceed as each member would report on his or her life, in particular on one's life in ministry. Usually the time would be shared equally. Sometimes an individual would need more time and would request that in advance or negotiate it during the meeting. Members would share facilitation, rotating the role weekly.

These groups serve as powerful centers of growth as people discover the challenge of defining ministry, the affirmation and stimulation that a group can offer, and the gratitude experienced in being able to support others. There is no substitute for having a group of people who expect to hear from us regularly about the conduct of our ministries, both in upholding us and in calling us forth. We become a microcosm of the church, the body of Christ.

The core group needs to become a support group. The task is complex, because in addition to its members supporting each other in individual ministries, this group is presumably carrying out a collective mission for change within the congregation. This requires more time and patience. But unless the core group members are well grounded in the reality of supporting each other in secular ministry, the group will be hard pressed to keep hold of the vision.

Once the core group has experienced itself as a support group, it might want to begin initiating other support groups. [2] A more simple step that the core group might want to propose first is that existing church committees begin with a time of personal sharing before starting on their common business. The members need not take more than a few minutes apiece, but if the sharing is focused and vulnerable— which needs to be modeled and which takes time to evolve— committees can become genuinely supportive. Furthermore, the committee work then takes place in the light of the other agendas of the members, which is a potent reality check. In addition, to begin meetings this way, while it requires thirty to forty-five minutes, greatly enhances the functioning of the group, because people have already been heard and so are prepared to lay aside their personal agendas that otherwise would inevitably find expression through the business.

4. Spiritual Formation

As individual members, we do not become one coordinated body automatically. Spiritual formation refers to the process by which we seek the Spirit's presence in order to become conformed to Christ. The Christian tradition testifies to the significance of the role of spiritual disciplines in this process. Following the physical analogy, conditioning is something to be engaged in over a lifetime. It is never complete; it always needs attending to; and it needs that attention on a daily basis.

Disciplines may be specially important for laity who move in a world that offers little confirmation of Christian identity or values. The daily work of formation is an ongoing reminder of ultimate allegiance. The exact habit that an individual or community adopts cannot be dictated. Nevertheless, there is some consensus within the Christian tradition that Scripture and prayer are basic. There are a number of lectionaries available that specify Scripture passages for each day and innumerable guides to prayer. What there may be less of is the number of invitations that direct us to Scripture, expecting, not timeless truth, but temporal patterns that can sensitize us to the shape of God's continuing action in our midst.

The tradition also advises us that disciplines are a communal enterprise. Our effort is to become the body, not to become spiritual stars. Other persons are not accidental to our formation; we are all flesh and blood together. Once again the core group is a place to begin the practice of disciplines, a daily time for reading Scripture and for prayer. The common disciplines become a resource in the group's life, offering a natural focus for centering and evolving as a shared experience.

Lectionaries can easily be shared in the church bulletin or other publications, and the whole congregation can be invited to join in the practice. It is especially helpful to provide opportunities for people to share their experience, lest a spirit of legalism arise. It is important to hear what kinds of growth and what kinds of problems individuals are experiencing. The disciplines invite us to fail, and that failure—whether a failure to follow the discipline or a failure to be illuminated by the content—is an essential part of the process.

Gifts and call, support and accountability, and spiritual formation form a natural trinity in that they are each an important element in the process of individuals' coming to identify and claim ministry. Each element has connections with the life of support groups. The following four items relate more to the congregational level of organization.

5. Language and Liturgy

The issues of sexism and language have sensitized many of us to the ways in which our common usage of words can either testify to new awareness or perpetuate old patterns. No one who has been exposed to the women's movement can hear "mankind" as an adequate term for humanity. In similar fashion, once we begin to recognize the ministry of the laity, our ears become alert in new ways. Does "minister" mean "ordained clergy"; is "ministry" being talked about as the work of the people or as the prerogative of professionals? And not language only, but also the forms of action in worship give evidence of deep structures of meaning. We are called to be a holy people, a royal priesthood, but in fact most of us let clergy stand proxy for us. As we begin to examine liturgy from these perspectives, we find ourselves asking these kinds of questions: who is doing the praying, the reading, the preaching, the consecrating and distributing, the confessing, and the forgiving? What world is being named, lifted up, hallowed? Whose ministry is being celebrated?

Each question implies directions for change. The changes surrounding language are simple, though not easily achieved. It is not difficult to use ministry inclusively, but old habits are difficult to alter. Liturgical change may be still more vigorously resisted—if the reasons for change are not well understood (and sometimes even if they are). But such public changes, when they can be implemented, have significant impact. Participation of the laity in the weekly service is a graphic witness to their priesthood. Of equal significance is attention to the secular world; mention of the work place in prayer and preaching; and lifting up the ministry of parenting, of friendship, of the stewardship of time. The aim is for the image of Romans 12 to take on flesh so that what we celebrate in worship really is the lifting up of our whole lives—and so that the act of worship, in turn, enables us to offer ourselves.

6. Validation

The recognition of the ministry of the laity occurs as individuals come to claim ministry; recognition also takes place in support groups. The question under consideration in respect to validation is recognition and affirmation of the ministry of the laity in the larger church context. Clergy have their ministries validated in a very specific manner: the act of ordination. Through this ritual the community testifies to their call to ministry, their preparation, and now their readiness to serve. The question, which George Peck has treated in his essay on call (see "The Call to Ministry"), is whether laity ought not to be similarly ordained, commissioned, or otherwise affirmed. In the absence of any public ritual, it is most difficult not to leave the impression that clergy are the "real" ministers.

Validation not only speaks within the community about who ministers, but it also offers individuals a very specific occasion for receiving support and for articulating the shape of long-range accountability. Jim Stockard in his essay "Commissioning the Ministries of the Laity" defined the effect on his ministry of his commissioning, indicating what a sustaining and inspirational force it has been for him.

The instituting of some form of liturgical validation is a major step that few congregations have taken. It raises profound and troubling questions: Do the clergy have a unique role that ought to be recognized by unique rituals? If laity are going to be ordained, who decides and on what basis? (Peck's essay also has suggestions here.) How many laity do we anticipate being ordained, and if it is less than all, what does that mean for the rest of the laity? These are questions without answers, for the time being. They are questions that a group, a task force, a board of deacons could decide to take up. Several of the essays in this volume would offer a starting point. The questions lead into the heart of the complexities that are inherent with the ministry of the laity. They challenge us to imagine how we might have to change if we were to embrace and embody this vision.

7. Education and Training

The educational mission of the church would be understood differently if we assumed that its major function was to equip laity for their ministry in the world. What are the tools, the resources, the skills that laity really need? How is the tradition best appropriated? What kind of Bible study is most helpful? It is of course laity who have to answer these questions. Few answers are known because few churches have invited laity to participate in this kind of dialogue.

A number of strategies that we have talked about thus far might fit under this heading. Consciousness raising, support group training, the use of the lectionary, and a study group on commissioning are all educational ventures. The key element in their success will probably be the extent to which the individuals involved in the planning have direct experience themselves with ministry in the secular arenas or the extent to which the planners are in partnership with those who have such experience. It may well be that those with the gifts and the time to plan the educational ministry will be focused on, and perhaps in the employ of, the institutional church. But if so, the involvement of laity who work in the world will be that much more indispensable.

The educational implications of the ministry of the laity are particularly interesting for younger people. The focus on equipping that we have been talking about has been with adults in mind. But the earlier emphasis on gifts and call has special relevance for youth. Why should the church leave vocational decisions to guidance counselors? The vision of every one of us called to full-time service ought to provide youth with a mandate that does not dictate the content of their choices but that does create expectations. In any work they are to be the stewards of their talents and their time. In any work how God is being loved and served is a critical question. In any work the perspectives of justice are obligatory. This mandate is going to make life difficult, but it is also going to make life adventuresome. If taken seriously the responsibilities of the community in representing this mandate could reshape the way in which we understand our work with youth.

8. Roles and Structures

The formation of a core group as a change strategy is a recognition of the critical function of structures and the roles that they define. In thinking about the local congregation from the point of view of the ministry of the laity, we ask ourselves "How does the way in which we are currently structured recognize and support the ministry of the laity?" For most of us the answers to this question are discouraging. Almost all of our church structures are devoted to the maintenance of the institution. Some may be focused on mission, some on the pastoral care of the congregation, but who in your congregation has responsibility for seeing that men and women are held accountable for and supported in the practice of their work place ministries? Your church is a rarity if you can point to a specific board or committee.

The first step in this examination of roles and structures is to begin to listen to the messages that our current patterns send out. If most of our structures are designed to serve the institution, that fact constitutes a loud message. If there is no explicit way in which laity are held accountable for ministry, that represents a loud silence. These structural communications, often because they are invisible, operate with great power. And there is power to be claimed in calling them into question.

With this level of change we are contemplating strategies that may take years to unfold. Institutions are rightly protective of their structures and resistant to seeing them altered. Any consideration of structural change needs to emerge as the culmination or ripening of an extensive project of education that will have made clear to a significant portion of the congregation why the changes are important. Indeed, unless a significant portion of the congregation has been involved in envisioning the changes, the changes will probably be resisted or ineffective if instituted.

Given the necessity of indigenous solutions, there is little to be said about the specific shape of structural changes other than to reaffirm their intended aim, which would be to organize the entire ministry of the congregation as an institution and as a body of ministers. That task will require new structures to take up the responsibilities now untouched and the realignment of existing structures to fit in with the new ones. A whole system will need to be recast.

This vision stretches ahead of us in incremental stages. Some steps are readily at hand. Any of us can begin to examine our lives and can begin to discern the shape of our ministries. Any of us can extend a call among our friends and create a group for support. The momentum for institutional change derives from these individual transformations. But there is an additional dimension of complexity involved in organizational change, and most of our strategies engage at that level. The difficulties that are inherent are worth the while and are part of the cost of faithful response. As covenantal people, we believe that God calls us into institutions, and we are called to reform those institutions so that they can be faithful agents. Laity are called to that task in the organizations that employ them. Laity and clergy are called to that task in reforming the church to be a servant body, a faithful institution that empowers the ministries of its members on behalf of a beloved world.

Notes

[1] There are many processes available. The laity project's is available from the Center for the Ministry of the Laity, at Andover Newton Theological School, Newton Centre, MA 02159.

[2] Resources for doing this are available from the Center.

Bibliography

Andover Newton Laity Project, *Covenanted Support for Ministry*.

Ayres, Francis, *The Ministry of the Laity*. Philadelphia: The Westminster Press, 1962.

Bucy, Ralph D., *The New Laity: Between Church and World*. Waco, Tex.: Word Press, 1978.

Campbell, Will D. and Holloway, James Y., *Callings*. Ramsey, N.J.: Paulist Press, 1974.

Childs, Marquis W. and Cater, Douglass, *Ethics in a Business Society*. New York: The New American Library, Inc., Mentor Press, 1973.

Come, Arnold, *Agents of Reconciliation*. Philadelphia: The Westminster Press, 1964.

Cosby, Gordon, *Handbook for Mission Support Groups*. Waco, Tex.: Word Press, 1975.

Diehl, William E., *Christianity and Real Life*. Philadelphia: Fortress Press, 1976.

————, *Thank God, It's Monday!* Philadelphia: Fortress Press, 1982.

Fenhagen, James C., *More Than Wanderers: Spiritual Disciplines for Christian Ministry*. New York: The Seabury Press, Inc., 1978.

————, *Mutual Ministry: New Vitality for the Local Church*. New York: The Seabury Press, Inc., 1977.

Gibbs, Mark and Morton, Ralph T., *God's Frozen People*. Philadelphia: The Westminster Press, 1965.

————— , *God's Lively People*. Philadelphia: The Westminster Press, 1971.

Greenleaf, Robert K., *Servant Leadership: A Journey into the Nature of Legitimate Power and Greatness*. New York: Paulist Press, 1977.

Hall, Cameron P., *Lay Action: The Church's Third Force*. New York: Friendship Press, 1974.

————— , *Listening to Lay People*. New York: Friendship Press. date unknown.

Kraemer, Hendrik, *A Theology of the Laity*. Philadelphia: The Westminster Press, 1958.

Littell, Franklin, and Hall, Cameron, *On the Job Ethics*. New York: National Council of Churches, Department of Economic Life, 1963.

Mouw, Richard, *Called to Holy Worldliness*. Edited by Mark Gibbs. Philadelphia: Fortress Press, 1980.

O'Connor, Elizabeth, *Eighth Day of Creation, Gifts and Creativity*. Waco, Tex.: Word Press, 1971.

————— , *Journey Inward, Journey Outward*. New York: Harper & Row, Publishers, Inc., 1975.

————— , *Our Many Selves*. New York: Harper & Row, Publishers, Inc., 1971.

Weber, Hans-Ruedi, *Living in the Image of Christ*. Valley Forge: Judson Press, 1986.

————— , *Salty Christians*. New York: The Seabury Press, Inc., 1963.

Wentz, Frederick, *Getting into the Act: Opening Up Lay Ministry in the Weekday World*. Nashville: Abingdon Press, 1978.

Whitehead, James D. and Evelyn E., *The Emerging Laity: Returning Leadership to the Community of Faith*. Garden City, N.Y.: Doubleday & Co., Inc., 1986.

Williams, Oliver F., *Full Value: Cases in Christian Business Ethics*. New York: Harper & Row, Publishers, Inc., 1978.

Index

Date Due

BRODART, INC. Cat. No. 23 233 Printed in U.S.A.